Peter Warren is a gifted communicator with a timely answer to one of life's biggest questions: "Why is there suffering in our world?" Many ask the question, "How I can make sense of my loved one getting cancer?" or, "If God is love, why does he allow calamities like war and natural disasters?" Peter has filled the pages of his book with clear and detailed responses to a host of such heartbreaking situations. His answers have come as he's struggled through his own headline grabbing tragedy. This book will be a great resource for people of faith who are looking for reasoned responses that will bring comfort to those torn by such suffering.

Pastor Bob Maddux
Trinity San Diego

When The Shooting Stopped is the most relevant book I have ever read on the subject of God and suffering. It's a book everyone should read, because every one of us has experienced some degree of suffering or loss in our lives. I found the principles and truths Peter Warren brings forth to be profound and life changing.

Sean Lambert
Founder
Homes of Hope

When the Shooting Stopped is a gift to all of us, but especially to those who have struggled with unanswered questions about pain and suffering. It is a subject many in the Western Christian World have put off as something that would never happen to a true believer. And then it does and we have no answers! I love the way Peter Warren takes us into his personal story and creates a feeling that we are there with him. However, he doesn't stop there. Just when you think there is no hope, he digs deep and brings clear and meaningful answers to the questions we all have. I highly recommend this book.

Dave Veach
Northwest District Supervisor
Foursquare International

As I began to read *When the Shooting Stopped*, I had a hard time putting it down. I went to bed reading it and had tears in my eyes when I came to the powerful ending the next day. This is not a read to be rushed through. Peter addresses the "hard questions" about our faith, God's character, and the evil we see in the world, in an understandable and engaging way. It will compel you to stop, ponder and wrestle through to conclusions that I trust will be foundational to your faith.

Darlene Cunningham
Co-founder
Youth With A Mission

D0063726

This book answers many of the questions Christians have about God's role in our lives and circumstances. As Peter wrestles with the heart of God—His love and mercy—in his own tragic situation, the question, "How could He?" becomes "How awesome is He!"

Jeffrey H. Coors
Chairman
Intercessors For America

"The truth of the nature and character of God shines through "When the Shooting Stopped" like a morning star. Peter Warren has lived this truth through painful experience and found wisdom, revelation, and understanding on the journey. His book is a must read for everyone looking for revelation in a world of pain and suffering."

Markus Steffen
International President
University of the Nations

Out of the depths of tragedy, evil and suffering Peter Warren brings to us biblical, philosophical, and practical truths to help us understand "Why bad things happen to good people." This is a great resource, a deep well of good counsel and advice. In one book you get a lot of answers to an age-old problem.

Dr Russ Frase
Founder
Joshua Nations

This could be one of the most important books that you ever read. Peter Warren had to lead his traumatized community into healing and hope. *When the Shooting Stopped* is that story. Peter's present convictions did not come easily. He and his friends faced agonizing circumstances that led to deep questions about the character of God. Keep this book near you for the rest of your life. From such suffering has come a deep exploration of its mysteries. Through these pages we are led to a place of comfort, but there are no shortcuts. This is a story that rings true; the illumination we need in this present darkness.

John Dawson
Founder
International Reconciliation Coalition

Thank you, Peter, for this masterpiece! You've done an amazing job showing the heart of God towards us in the face of suffering. I love the way you continually go back to His Word for perspective. It's a powerful reminder that God is always with us, especially in those times when we struggle to make sense of situations that make no sense at all.

Bishop Israel Ade-Ajala
Kingdom Connection Christian Center
Aurora, Colorado

Thank you Peter for tackling a topic many of us have no words for. The clarity with which you write gives readers a new perspective, and challenges what many of us have come to believe about God's hand in our world. Your book is not just a reflection on your own personal experience, but also, a thorough theological exploration on the topic of suffering. As believers we all need this type of framework for our faith amidst difficult circumstances. *When the Shooting Stopped* provides this framework and gives wisdom and strength to press through and help others on the other side."

Ryan Malouff
Lead pastor
Expression Church, Austin, Texas

Wonderfully done, passionately expressed, and carefully constructed, *When the Shooting Stopped* gripped my heart from the first page! The book appeals not only to the searching heart that wonders about how God interacts with His creation, but also to leaders who want a solid Biblical foundation as they grapple with the issues of human suffering. When tragedy struck the YWAM base in Denver (a place I love and have frequently visited), Peter Warren's heart turned in the right direction! His purposeful seeking after the Lord resulted in a finished product that will resonate in the Body of Christ for ages. Thank you Peter for laying out your discoveries in the chapters of this incredible book!

Pastor Jack Hempfling
Regional Director
Elim Fellowship, LeRoy, New York

This is a must read. The knowledge and revelation Peter has gained through his years of ministering to others is all wrapped up in this book. It is a wealth of wisdom and encouragement for anyone at any season of life.

Pastor Greg DeVries
The Well, Scottsboro Alabama

The wisdom Peter shares in response to life's most difficult questions will be a great benefit to both individuals and small groups.

Maureen Menard
YWAM Centre for Discipleship Training Schools

Peter draws from his deep personal understanding of God's character in the aftermath of his own tragic experience, to address the age-old question, "Why do the innocent suffer?" He does so with astonishing clarity. He has spoken often in our training classes, and this book adds a valuable tool for our Hope Force Reservists who must deal with tragic loss on a consistent basis as they minister in the aftermath of disasters around the world.

Jack and Cherie Minton
Founders, Hope Force International

Thank you, Peter, for venturing into one of the most perplexing arenas that theologians and philosophers have attempted to solve for years—the issue of evil and suffering. Without resorting to one-liners or cute religious clichés, and without going to extremes either on the sovereignty of God or the reality of spiritual warfare, you share biblical insights from your own life with great clarity and insight. Thank you.

Danny Lehmann
Evangelist and author

"In this book, my friend Peter wrestles thoughtfully with some of the hardest questions which human beings ever have to face—questions having to do with unexpected suffering and terrible injustice. He writes not from the comfort of an abstract, philosophical armchair, but as one who was impacted deeply, personally, experientially by a horrific tragedy—a tragedy that no one should ever have to face.

Peter does not gloss over the issues of pain with religious platitudes, but he sets his heart to explore honestly how we confront evil in a broken world. As you journey with him through these pages you will be challenged to think through cultural presuppositions and embrace biblical attitudes which make room for forgiveness and redemption. It won't be an easy journey, but it is not one we can simply wish away. I urge you to wrestle with these issues along with Peter and discover for yourself a fresh foundation for trusting God in the midst of difficult circumstances.

David Joel Hamilton
Vice President for Strategic Innovation
YWAM's University of the Nations"

"'Why?' It is the question every one of us is tempted to ask when we face circumstances that don't make sense or seem unfair. Why did I get sick? Why did I lose my job? Why is this happening to our family? Why did two young adults, preparing to serve God, have to lose their lives in a senseless act of violence? It doesn't make sense. And, where is God in the midst of all of this? In this book, Peter has created a thorough, theological framework, with the backdrop of his own personal story of tragedy, to help us wrestle with the concepts of the sovereignty of God, mans free will, fairness and justice. Though knowing 'why' is not a guarantee of peace, understanding who God is and how He loves us does encourage the human heart and gives us the ability to trust God even when we struggle to understand the 'why?'"

Pastor David Zetterberg
Oasis Church, Lakewood Washington

WHEN THE SHOOTING STOPPED

Where is God When We Suffer?

FOREWORD BY LOREN CUNNINGHAM

WHEN THE SHOOTING STOPPED

PETER WARREN

Where is God When We Suffer?

When the Shooting Stopped: Where is God when we suffer?
Copyright © 2019 by Peter Warren

ISBN: 978-1-7343205-0-3 (paperback)
ISBN: 978-1-7343205-1-0 (ebook)

Printed in the United States of America

DEDICATED TO
PHILIP CROUSE AND
TIFFANY JOHNSON

ACKNOWLEDGMENTS

I owe a debt of gratitude to many people for their hand in helping bring this book to life.

First of all I thank my YWAM Denver family for their encouragement and continual support during the three long years of this project. I especially want to thank Cailyn Vargas, Jordyn Russnogle and Lauren Kuerbis for the extra hours put in to get us across the finish line.

I thank Rachel Harrison, Jack Hempfling, Bob Maddux and Mary Cooney for their intelligent critiques and for offering a slightly different perspective on several points that helped stretch my thinking in important ways.

I am grateful to Chief Don Wick, Deputy Chief A.J. DeAndrea, Police Commander Bob VanderVeen, and the entire Arvada Police Department for their professionalism and quick response the night of the shootings.

I thank Jeff and Lis Coors, Heath and Rebecca Cardie, Craig and Lisa Ambler and David and Betsy Zahniser for believing in this project and for their valuable partnership.

I thank the members of my intercessory team who provided an ongoing prayer shield for me as I wrote the manuscript: Allysen George, Carol Gale, Charis Jackson, Chase Adams, Colin Johnson, Dale Mast, David Stabler, Deena Craig, Diana Bergstrom, Donna Livingston, Evelyn McHugh, Heather Hall, Heidi Zeiner, Janet Butler, Jason Jasasra, Jeff Ryan, Jennifer Patterson, Jennifer Russnogle, Jodi Brown, John and Michele Copeland, Jonathan Weister, Julianne af Petersens, Karen Silva, Kellie Wiliams, Kit Hackett, Linda Palmer, Marcela Almeida, Mark Anderson, Mary Homesly, Melissa Matthias, Nynke Arends, Pat Eachus, Ralph

Harris, Rebekah Frost, Rick Joyce, Ro'i and Laurel Steiner, and Trish Webster. Every book is a team effort, and your part has been invaluable.

I am grateful to those who gave me permission to share from their perspective: Stephanie Snell, Keely Lange, Amanda Bower, Jisook Han, Naomi Gill, Mindy Berry, John Murphy, Paul Dangtoumda and Joshua Bergen. This book is their story too.

I owe a debt of gratitude to Marcia Zimmermann, Carol Saia and Donna MacGowan whose superb editing and valuable insights helped further my thinking and produce the final outcome.

I thank my writing coach Scott Tompkins, whose wisdom and professionalism helped fine tune (and almost cut in half) the original manuscript. I'll always remember your constant advice: "Keep chipping away at the marble until you reach the hidden figure within."

I will be forever indebted to Allison Ngo, my personal assistant, for her long hours of hard work and dedication to me personally, and for always pushing me to keep the project on target.

I am grateful to my father and mother, Rix and Irma Warren, who taught me to never give up in the face of impossible circumstances.

I thank my Personal Band of Brothers, Sean Lambert, Michael Berg, Dave Stone, Danny Lehmann, David Hamilton, and Markus Steffen, for their ongoing support and inspiration.

And finally, I thank Linda Warren, my life partner and best friend, for inspiring me, for being my most severe critic, and for her unyielding belief in me.

Answering life's most painful question

By Loren Cunningham
Co-founder of Youth With A Mission

Over the last six decades, as I have ministered in every nation of the world, I discovered that young people, especially in universities, ask the same question: "If God is a God of love, why do the innocent suffer?"

Every generation has faced the question of suffering and injustice. To most people, some pain seems merited. They see it as the undesirable—but expected—consequence of wrong choices and actions. That suffering may seem appropriately just, but why do those who have done no wrong suffer? Why does tragedy occur to those who do not merit it? Does God want the innocent to suffer? Does he orchestrate it? Or is God broken-hearted by it? If so, why does God allow injustice and suffering to go on? If he's all-powerful, why doesn't God stop it? If he's all-loving, why does God let injustice and suffering exist at all?

These age-old questions grip the human heart every time unexplainable tragedy crushes us. Bad things happen to good people. This is what we see. This is what we experience. When disease and death, pain and poverty, sickness and sorrow, tragedy and tumult disrupt our lives, everything within us wants to scream, "No! It should not be so." We weep and ask, "Where is God when life hurts?"

The Book of Job, which scholars believe is the first written book of the Bible, honestly grapples with the problem of undeserved pain. In Job, there is no skirting of the issues, no avoiding of the implications. Job's story presents suffering and injustice powerfully and poignantly. It does not gloss over the reality of pain, and it does not leave us without hope. "Job's agonized search for real answers amidst terrible pain leads to a transformational encounter with God. His dramatic experience brings us face-to-face with the God who holds the answers to our most profound questions."[1]

The book you now hold in your hands is a contemporary book of Job. My dear friend Peter and the many others affected by the tragic shooting in Denver suffered greatly. How could this have happened? Why did this happen? Where was God amidst all of this? As Peter wrestles with these complicated questions, this event will grip your heart, exercise your mind, and finally challenge your will. Like Job, Peter pulls no punches. This story has no fairy tale ending, but you will see hope arise from tragedy and redemption from injustice.

But be warned. To read this book well, you must be willing to face the hard questions. Honestly. And you must be open to the answers. Like Job's friends, too many of us have believed in simplistic caricatures of God, which dull our senses as we go about our daily lives. But tragedy—unexpected, unjust tragedy—can awaken us to fresh insight. That is if we don't give up. As Job said to God, at the end of his long ordeal, "I had only heard about you before, but now I have seen you with my own eyes."[2]

Like the book you hold in your hands, the Bible is honest, brutally honest. It points out time and again that good people do experience bad things. For most religious people and systems, this is unsettling. Subsequently, they either explain away innocence, or they justify suffering. Not so in the Bible. It presents human life with all its potential and pain. Though the suffering of innocents was not a part of God's original plan, the Bible gives answers about why this has happened. The Bible also tells us that this tragic situation will not go on forever. A day is coming when "there will be no more death or sorrow or crying or pain. All these things are gone forever."[3]

What brought about this change? What made the difference? God stepped into our world. His son Jesus, the most innocent of all, suffered more than all, so that all of us who are not at all innocent, might never have to suffer again. This is an incredible story. And it's real. It's raw. It's true.

Therefore, read on. Read this book. Read the Bible. And as you read, keep your heart and mind open so that you, like Job, can see God as you've never seen him before.

TABLE OF CONTENTS

INTRODUCTION

The terrifying wave of school shootings across America has now planted in the minds of every teacher and administrator the idea that it could happen to them. They hope and pray it won't. They process how they might respond if it did. But no one knows the answer to that question until a shooting happens at their school, as it did at mine on December 9, 2007.

Ours is not a typical school. I lead the Youth With A Mission (YWAM) center in Denver, where we offer Christian discipleship training programs for young adults. We teach them how to develop a personal relationship with God, and we send them out from our training centers (called bases) to share love and faith with others around the world. So when a former student randomly fired upon our staff and students that cold night, it rocked my world in more ways than I can describe.

I began to question why a God of love would allow such a tragedy. I had grown up believing he was just and loving, yet the seeming injustice of what happened was a challenge to my faith. I needed to wrap my mind around it, or at least come to a place where I was at peace in my own heart. I had, on numerous occasions, counseled others who had also encountered tragedy—the death of a loved one or some personal misfortune like an accident or a natural disaster.

Why didn't God intervene? This was their question too. Certainly God is powerful enough, and yet he had seemingly done nothing. Was it because he didn't care? Or was he actually the one orchestrating events from behind the scenes? That was what some people were telling us. If either conclusion was true, it would raise serious questions about the character of a God who claims to be, righteous in all his ways and kind in all his works (Ps. 145:17). But I wanted to find out for myself, even if the truth turned out to be painful. So I embarked on a journey that led me to write this book.

I challenge you to approach the following chapters with an open mind and a teachable heart. If you disagree with my conclusions when you're done, that's fine, but maybe you will see things in a different light. I examine ten contexts in which suffering occurs in our world and what the Bible has to say about each one of them. I believe God isn't displeased by hard questions. He told Jeremiah, "You will seek me and find me, when you seek me with all your heart" (Jer. 29:13).

Most importantly, my purpose in writing this book is not to impose my theological conclusions on anyone. It is simply to share my heart and the lessons learned from the tragic events at YWAM Denver on December 9, in 2007. I have endeavored to base all my research and conclusions on the Bible, which I consider to be the Word of God, yet after twelve years of in-depth study, questions remain. I realize that if one embarks on a journey to understand God completely, they will never reach their destination. Some things are beyond the scope of human comprehension. Nevertheless, I continue in a relentless pursuit of God, knowing that one day everything will make perfect sense when I see him face-to-face (1 Cor. 13:12).

"And you will know the truth, and the truth will set you free."

—Jesus

"The truth will set you free, but first it will p*ss you off."

—Joe Klass, *Twelve Steps to Happiness*

"The pure and simple truth is rarely pure and never simple."

—Oscar Wilde

"Intense feeling too often obscures the truth."

—President Harry S. Truman

"Cry out for insight and ask for understanding. Search for them as you would for silver; seek them like hidden treasures."

—King Solomon

"You can be standing right in front of the truth and not necessarily see it, and people only get it when they're ready to get it."

—George Harrison, *The Beatles Anthology*

CHAPTER ONE

There's been a shooting at the base

*In this world you will have trouble. But take
heart! I have overcome the world.*

—JESUS

It was a cold December evening shortly after midnight. I had
been asleep for several hours when I was awakened by the
incessant ringing of our doorbell. I stumbled out of bed and
from my bedroom door I could see my son, Stephen, opening
the door. In came two of our YWAMers, and one of them,
Anthony Lee, blurted out words I'll never forget. "There's been
a shooting at the base."

I was trying to wrap my mind around what I had just heard
when my daughter, Rachel, burst out of her bedroom. "Dad,
it's Tiffany," she said. And then she mentioned some other
names of people who had been shot. I ran back into my bedroom, threw on whatever clothes I could find, and rushed out
to my car. Stephen and Rachel followed. It had been snowing
lightly and four or five inches had accumulated on the roof and

windshield. We brushed it off as best we could and sped over to the YWAM base, four blocks away.

When we arrived, it was like something from a movie scene. The parking lot was full of ambulances and police cars, all with their lights flashing. Everything was reflecting off the freshly fallen snow, and the driveway had been cordoned off with yellow police tape. An officer approached the car as I drove up. He lifted his rifle and pointed it right at me, motioning for me to back away. I stopped and poked my head out of the driver side window.

"I'm the ministry leader here, please let us through."

"I don't care. Get out of here," he said.

I could see I wasn't going to be able to reason with him, so I backed up and drove over to the Safeway parking lot across the street.

Three blocks away, Kevin Verrone and John Murphy were up late playing video games in Kevin's basement when they got the call. They threw on their coats and rushed outside, coming face-to-face with a stranger in a long dark trench coat. As their eyes met, the young man slipped on a patch of ice and fell hard to the ground.

"Are you okay, man?" John asked, but the stranger did not answer. He just got up and scurried off down the hill with his head down. It wasn't until later they realized they had come face-to-face with the shooter. He was headed southward, away from the base, although we found out later his vehicle was parked in the same parking lot where Stephen, Rachel, and I were waiting. According to police detective Bob VanDerVeen, the cell towers put Matthew Murray back at the parking lot across from the base until he drove away at 1:25AM.

The phone startled me as we sat waiting. It was my wife, Linda. "They're taking them to Saint Anthony's," she said. "Swing by the house and pick me up." The four of us drove 15 minutes away to Saint Anthony's Hospital, still not fully aware of the enormity of what had just happened. We hurried into the emergency room. As we were checking in, the chaplain on duty came over to introduce himself. He told us two of our YWAMers had been brought in, but the others were taken to Denver Central. By this time, we had heard four had been shot, but we did not know why or by whom. The chaplain took us back to one of the hospital rooms where Charlie Blanch was awake. He had been shot in the legs but was fully alert and able to tell us what had happened.

The chaplain identified the other person they had brought in as Tiffany Johnson. She was the head of our YWAM hospitality department, and a close friend of our family. He told us he saw Tiffany giving a description of the shooter as the paramedics wheeled her into the emergency room. That is when I decided to call her parents.

A PHONE CALL I WISH I'D NEVER MADE

Tom and Diane Johnson had already heard about the shootings but seemed grateful I had called them. I repeated what the chaplain told me. It is a phone call I wish I had never made. Her dad's response still haunts me. He said, "Tiff's a fighter. If she was awake and talking, I know she's going to pull through." She didn't.

Around 3:00 AM, Linda and I looked up to see the chaplain walking down the hallway toward us. He had a troubled look on his face. "Tiffany didn't make it," he mumbled, as if he still didn't believe it himself. "The surgeon said she went into cardiac arrest on the operating table, and they couldn't save her. Unbeknown to the first responders, a bullet had grazed the vena cava, and she'd been bleeding internally the whole time."

I was stunned. Didn't they tell us an hour ago she was alert and talking? This couldn't be happening. But it was. One of the hardest things I have ever done was call her parents again to tell them their daughter had passed away.

IT WAS THE DIFFERENCE BETWEEN LIFE AND DEATH

By now it was almost daybreak. Four of our YWAMers had been shot—Philip Crouse, Dan Griebenow, Charlie and Tiffany, all young people who had come to YWAM Denver to get closer to God. Someone at Denver Central told us Dan was going to pull through despite taking a bullet to the neck, but Phil was not so fortunate. Three bullets hit him as he dove for cover. One of them took his life.

All of it seemed so random. Charlie and Phil both dove for cover through adjacent doors that exited the hallway. One opened outward and the other inward. The detectives told me later this was the difference between life and death. Charlie's door opened away from the corridor, allowing him to jump out of harm's way, whereas Phil's opened outward, exposing his entire body to the spray of bullets coming down the hallway. Another baffling fact was that Phil was over thirty feet from the shooter, whereas Dan was standing right in front of him when he opened fire. How did Dan survive? Was it just a fluke the bullet missed his windpipe, spinal cord, and jugular vein, or was there some other explanation?

If you have ever experienced personal tragedy, the first question you ask is, "Why?" If you believe in God, that question will undoubtedly be directed at him. "Why would you allow this to happen, Lord," I prayed, "especially to two young missionaries whose only ambition was to serve you? Were they just in the wrong place at the wrong time, or is there some higher purpose I don't yet understand?" There were no good answers. Everything seemed so painfully confusing. Most of all, it seemed so unjust, especially for the two who lost their lives and the loved ones they left behind.

HE WAS SOMEONE WE KNEW

The gunman had escaped, and our northwest Denver community was on high alert. That afternoon we heard there had been another shooting at a church seventy miles away in Colorado Springs. Some were speculating it might be a copycat shooter, but it wasn't. It was the same person, and I would soon discover he was someone we knew.

Our base was still an active crime scene, so we decided to move our workers and students to our mountain camp, Eagle Rock. Our leaders felt it was important to gather the whole group to share what we knew, to process it and to pray.

As I was on my way, a call came in from a friend who pastors a church in the city. Phil Abeyta was one of the first guys I met when we moved to Colorado in 1984. He was usually upbeat and positive, but I could tell something was bothering him. What he told me hit me like a ton of bricks. "Peter," he paused, "the shooter was my nephew, Matthew Murray. He did a Discipleship Training School (DTS) at your base five years ago. He's the one who shot people in The Springs also. I'm so sorry, brother, I don't know what to say."

'CHRISTIAN AMERICA, THIS IS YOUR COLUMBINE'

Matthew Murray had been raised in a loving home, but never felt fully accepted by Christians outside his own family. His parents tried to involve him in Christian youth programs such as ours, but his sense of isolation and loneliness deepened. In his early twenties, he started attending Saturday night mass at *Ordo Templi Orientis,* an occult group associated with the teachings of Aleister Crowley. He would also post regular blogs on the *Ex-Pentecostals* forum, expressing his hatred toward Christians.

Matthew was enrolled as a DTS student at our base, but his outreach leaders did not want him to go with the class on their field assignment to Bosnia and Herzegovina because of his increasingly erratic behavior and disregard for school guidelines.

The anger in Matthew's heart had been simmering below the surface for some time, and it was about to boil over. A year earlier, New Life Church in Colorado Springs split apart after their pastor was dismissed because of an alleged affair with a prostitute. The story went viral, and Matthew was deeply impacted by this incident because he had attended New Life on several occasions with his mom. It seemed that this was the final straw, and he felt he needed to do something about it. Something big. Something everyone would remember.

According to the police report, Matthew had been reading books on Witchcraft, Freemasonry, the works of Aleister Crowley, and Adolf Hitler's *Mein Kampf.* He was fascinated with the Platte Canyon High School hostage incident in 2006 and the Columbine High School massacre in 1999. There were over two terabytes of information stored on his computer including explanatory notes on "Practical Homicide," and "How to Survive a Tactical Shooting." All this clearly was pushing Matthew closer and closer to the edge.

He decided to settle accounts first with his current "church." On the evening of December 8th, he drove to the Metaphysical Research Society facility where *Ordo Templi Orientis* was holding their Saturday evening mass. According to police detective, Bob VanDerVeen, "they had told Matthew to stay away because of his erratic behavior, but unbeknownst to him, the location of the meeting had been changed."[1] So there he was, armed with his weapons, but locked out. That is when he got back into his car and drove to the YWAM campus.

In the fourteen hours between the two massacres, he went online. "You Christians are all gonna die," he posted. "You brought this on yourselves." And then later, "I'm coming for EVERYONE soon and I WILL be armed to the (expletive) teeth and I WILL shoot to kill … I can't wait till I can kill you people. I feel no remorse, no sense of shame, I don't care if I live or die in the shoot-out. All I want to do is kill and injure as many of you as I can, especially Christians who are to blame for most of the problems in the world."[2] And then, finally, "Christian America, this is YOUR Columbine."[3] That was the last thing he ever wrote. The statement was posted at 10:03 AM on December 9th under the name *nghtmrchid26*, but it later came to light he had written it two days earlier. He also had video footage of the interior of the YWAM building, including the hallway where the shootings took place.

This raises a question that still baffles many of those involved in the situation. Why did Matthew go off the deep end? He had a family who loved him. His dad is one of the kindest men I know, a neurologist who has devoted the bulk of his career to research a cure for Multiple Sclerosis. His mom is the type of person with whom everyone feels comfortable, and he was raised in a warm, wholesome environment with a sister and brother who turned out just fine. But Matthew was different.

"There was something unsettling about him," recalled Keeley Lange, one of his fellow DTS students. Some of his roommates reported he would sometimes talk in strange voices, and one time started crawling upside-down like the girl in the spider scene from *The Exorcist*. That really freaked them out. "When the shooting was over, I felt really bad," Keeley added. "I couldn't help wondering if there was something I could have done that would have changed the way things turned out. But now I'll never know."[4]

TIFFANY SAVED MANY LIVES

Matthew arrived at our center a little before midnight and parked just north of the campus. He made his way to the main entrance, but there was a problem. The doors had been locked for the night. He knocked several times but to no avail. Then suddenly, the door opened.

Stephanie Snell was surprised when she did not recognize Matthew. Some of the students had gone out bowling, and she thought he was one of them. He told her not to worry because he had been given permission to stay for the night. It was a lie. The detectives told me later he was planning a massacre. He had stockpiled a cache of arms including a Bushmaster XM-15 which he had modified to allow a larger caliber round, a Beretta .40 semi-automatic handgun, a Beretta .22 caliber handgun, a Springfield Armory 9mm semi-automatic pistol, and an AK-47 assault rifle. He had over 2,000 rounds of ammunition which had been delivered by mail to his parents' home in the Denver suburb of Englewood. There were 65 staff and students living in the building at the time he gained access. Detectives believe his plan was to go from room to room to shoot as many people as possible.

Stephanie told Matthew to wait while she went to look for Tiffany, but Tiffany was gone. She had decided to spend the night at a friend's house and would not be back till morning. "Something was off with him," she told me later. "He asked where the bathroom was, and after he didn't come back for a while, I went upstairs to get ready for bed. I felt so uneasy the whole time I decided I had to try and find Tiffany one last time, and this time I found her."[5] Tiffany's friend had come down with a cold so she decided to come back to the base.

Matthew told Tiffany that my wife, Linda, had given him permission to stay for the night. "Well," Tiffany responded, "Linda didn't say anything to me, and I'm not going to call her after midnight to verify this. So I'm sorry, but you're going to have to make alternate plans."

That one decision, denying Matthew permission to stay for the night, is what saved the lives of many others. It was a decision, however, that cost Tiffany her own life. Our police chief, Don Wick, said in his last public statement about the shootings: "Tiffany saved many lives."

THE DOOR THAT WOULD NEVER SHUT, SHUT

Tiffany's boyfriend, Dan, and two of the other staff guys had been playing video games in the men's dorm when they stopped to help Tiffany escort Matthew from the premises. After showing him to the side door, they turned to walk back. Suddenly, what sounded like fireworks erupted in the hallway, but it wasn't fireworks. It was the rapid succession of rounds being fired from Matthew's 9mm semi-automatic pistol. Dan Griebenow was shot twice, once in the neck and once in the shoulder. Charlie Blanch was struck two times in his legs. Phillip Crouse suffered three gunshot wounds—two to his torso and one to his leg. Tiffany Johnson was shot twelve times, bullets hitting her hand, wrist, face, legs, and torso. Student Stephen Long was observing the interaction with Matthew from the doorway of his dorm room. When the firing erupted, he dove back inside, and then tried to flee out the bedroom window, but to no avail.[6] He probably would have been next, except that Matthew stepped outside—apparently to reload his weapons—and got locked out.

The west-side door that opened to the parking lot was a commercial-grade steel door that had always been a problem. We had had it serviced numerous times, but it still would never close unassisted. You had to give it a firm tug or it would remain ajar, but not on this night. The door that would never shut, shut, and locked Matthew out. It appears he had put his foot in the door to keep it open while he reloaded, but his foot must have slipped, and the door closed and locked in front of him. How it shut on its own is a mystery to all of us. To our knowledge, it had never done that before.

At that exact moment, several of our YWAM guys were returning from a concert and heard the gunshots. When they entered the parking lot, they could see Matthew peering through the security glass and tugging on the door to try to get back in. When he turned and saw them, he ran away.

THIS MIGHT BE MY FINAL MOMENT

The next few hours were surreal. The police arrived less than two minutes after the first 911 call. They were surgical in their approach. They had learned from Columbine to take charge and go in, rather than giving the perpetrator time to plot his next move. The SWAT Team surrounded the premises and moved in, ready to confront whatever was inside.

YWAMers were scattered throughout the 17,000-square-foot building, hiding behind desks, under beds, and in closets. Naomi Gill was in her bedroom right above the hallway when the shots rang out. "I immediately thought of my family back in England," she told me. "I remember desperately trying to call them and tell them how much I loved them. I will never forget the sheer horror of that moment as we barricaded ourselves in our room, thinking that we were going to be next."[7]

Tiffany's roommate, Amanda Lange, was already in bed for the night. "I was dozing off when suddenly I heard what sounded like fireworks," she said. "The next thing I knew, one of the staff girls, Holly, opened the door and told me to call 911. 'Those were gunshots!' she shouted and then ran off.

"When I got through to the dispatcher, she told me to stay put. I kept wondering where would the safest place be to hide. The dispatcher was telling me there were others calling too, and then I heard someone running down the hallway and banging on the door. I assumed the worst. I wondered if this might be my final moment. But it was one of the staff guys checking to see if everyone was okay."

"I stayed on the phone with the dispatcher for a while longer, and then decided to call my fiancé, Peter Bower. I was still on the phone with him when the SWAT Team burst through the door. They pointed their guns right at me and asked if I was the only one in the room. Finally, they escorted me downstairs, guns still drawn. That's when I saw the blood by the pay phone where Charlie had been standing. I wondered if anyone had been killed. The police corralled us all into the foyer, and it was strange because some of the guys had been handcuffed and were sitting there with the rest of us. Everything was so confusing, and I could tell the others were scared too."[8]

One of our young Korean women, Jisook Han, had been in the bathroom adjacent to the hallway where the shooting took place. "On my way there, I remember seeing a guy talking on the phone," she told me later. "He was looking at the pictures on the wall and I assumed he was a visitor. Later, I could hear people talking in the hallway. Then without warning, there was a loud banging. The bathroom door flung open and Charlie burst in. I could hear screaming in the hallway. Charlie stood up and immediately ran back out again. Then, I heard someone calling 911. That's when I realized it was shooting I had heard. I didn't know what to do so I hid in one of the shower stalls. I thought someone was going to come in at any moment and shoot me. I felt numb and dizzy all over. The next thing I knew, a policeman was flinging open the curtain and pointing at me with his gun. I was horrified, but at the same time so relieved to see him."[9]

CANINE SEARCH

While all this was happening on the inside, officers were conducting a canine search throughout the neighborhood around the base. They hoped footprints in the freshly fallen snow might lead them to the suspect, but they didn't. Commander A.J. DeAndrea drove his patrol car over to my house, four blocks away, and found the front door wide open. "You scared me to death," he told me later. "When I saw the open door, my first thought was the shooter had gone to your place next."[10] Thankfully, it was a false alarm. In our haste to get to the hospital we must have failed to close the door properly, and it had blown open in the storm.

A reverse 911 call was issued to alert our neighborhood that a shooter was on the loose, but by this time Matthew was long gone. He had zigzagged through backyards, climbing over fences, and doubling back to cover his tracks. He even went up to someone's front door and then backed away, making it look like he had entered there. All the neighborhood dogs were inside because of the subfreezing temperatures, which helped make his escape easier. When he finally got to his car, he drove home undetected. His getaway plan had worked exactly as planned. A few hours later he headed to Colorado Springs and gunned down two young sisters at New Life church before an armed guard shot him and ended his murderous spree.

THE INTERROGATION

In the early morning hours, everyone at the base was rounded up and shuttled down to the police station "We were taken just as we were," said one of the students, "some in pajamas, and others in t-shirts and bare feet. We were interrogated one by one, and no one was allowed to talk to anyone else because the police weren't sure if someone was in collusion with the shooter. Then, at daybreak, they suddenly told us we were free to go."

Since we couldn't return to the base, we piled into vans and headed up to Eagle Rock. By mid-morning, everyone had heard Tiffany and Philip had passed away. It was a hard pill to swallow. We had just been with them at our Christmas party, fifteen hours earlier, and now they were gone ... forever. How could this happen, and, most of all, why didn't God prevent it from happening?

PERSONAL APPLICATION

With this overview, then, let's take a deep breath and plunge headfirst into the challenging task of answering the question: If God is just and loving, as the scriptures tell us, why is there so much suffering in the world he created? As anyone who has encountered tragedy will tell you, there are no simple answers. But answers exist, right in the middle of God's Word.

Before we begin, however, there are two important questions I want to ask you:

In what ways have you experienced suffering in your life?

Sadly, suffering touches all of us. It's part of the human condition. Families suffer when there is an accident, or a fatal illness takes the life of a beloved family member. Organizations suffer when conflict tears apart what was once a peaceful workplace, or when the company goes bankrupt. Entire communities suffer when there is a national tragedy, like war or a natural disaster. None of us are exempt from suffering, as Jesus pointed out to his disciples: "In the world you will have tribulation," he told them (John 16:33). How we handle suffering however, especially in our relationship with God, is of utmost importance.

How has suffering impacted the way you relate to God?

It's easy to blame God when we suffer, especially if we've been taught that everything that happens on earth is his will. In the following chapters I want to challenge that notion. And just to be clear, although the shootings provide a useful starting point for our discussion, the event itself is not the sole purpose of this book. My goal is to shed light on why suffering occurs in our world, and God's role in it. We must leave no stone unturned in our relentless pursuit of the truth. As President John Quincy Adams once said: "It is by a thorough knowledge of the whole subject that people are enabled to judge the past correctly and give a proper direction to the future."

CHAPTER TWO

Selfishness

*Suffering is the price that had to be paid for
love and freedom to exist at all.*

—C. S. LEWIS

There is no denying God does not intervene every time we do something foolish, or unloving, or when we make selfish choices that cause others to suffer. He could have created mindless automatons over which he would have complete control, but instead, he created humans with the freedom to love and obey him … or not. Selfishness, unfortunately, is the inevitable byproduct of the freedom we've been given.

This was the issue our community was grappling with in the days following the shootings. Why didn't God stop Matthew Murray as he drove to YWAM on that cold, December night? Surely, he could have made his car slide off the road in the snowstorm or caused him to have a flat tire somewhere along the way. Some have argued that if God were truly just, he would ensure that no injustices ever occurred. He would either override man's selfish choices, or better still, cause him to experience the same degree of pain he was inflicting on others. That would be the ultimate deterrent, wouldn't it? Not really. Think about it for a moment. What would this world of perfect fairness really be like? It would actually create an environment conducive to even greater selfishness.

Author Philip Yancey argues that in such a perfectly fair world, morality would have to operate according to fixed laws, just like the laws of nature. Punishment for wrongdoing would work like physical pain. If you touch a flame, you are punished instantly with a pain warning; a fair world would punish sin just as swiftly and surely. Extend your hand to shoplift, and you'd get an electrical shock. Likewise, a fair world would reward good behavior: Fill out your taxes honestly, and you'd earn a pleasure sensation, like a trained seal given a fish.

That imaginary world has a certain appeal doesn't it? It would be just and consistent, and everyone would know exactly what God expected. Fairness would reign. There is, however, one huge problem with such a tidy world: it's not at all what God wanted to accomplish when he put man on earth. He wants from us love, freely given love, and we dare not underestimate the premium he places on that love. Freely given love is so important to God that he allows our planet to be a cancer of evil in his universe—for a time.

If the world ran according to fixed, perfectly fair rules, there would be no true freedom. We would act rightly because of our own immediate gain, and selfish motives would taint every act of goodness. We would love God because of a programmed, inborn hunger, not because of a deliberate choice in the face of attractive alternatives.[1]

God did not stop Matthew Murray as he drove to YWAM that night because Matthew was created with the God-given ability to make his own decisions in life. The same freedom that gave him the ability to love was what gave him the ability to be selfish and violent. If God were to eliminate all the suffering born from man's abuse of his freedom, he would also be eliminating man's ability to love, which was the whole reason he created us in the first place.

CREATED FOR LOVE

At the beginning of the human race, God created man *like* himself. The Bible records his exact words: "Let us make man in our image, after our likeness" (Gen. 1:26). But what does that mean? The truth is, we are not that similar to God. He is all-powerful, all-present, and all-knowing, and he has no beginning or end. We, on the other hand, have limited power and knowledge, we can only be in one place at a time, and our existence can be traced back to a specific chronological point. And yet, the Bible tells us we were made in the image of God. How then? The answer must be, can only be, that we were made *like* God according to his personality rather than his nature. We have intellect, emotions, and a free will. That's what makes a person a person. God possesses these attributes and so do we. It's not because he is like us, but because we are like him.

God's personality is revealed in his interactions with man. On one occasion he said to his friend Isaiah, "Come now, let us reason together" (Isa. 1:18). Could this really be what God meant to say? Did he actually intend for Isaiah to interact with him on an intellectual level? There seems to be no other way to accurately interpret this passage. And wasn't that what Abraham did when he prayed for Sodom and Gomorrah? He reasoned that it would be unjust if God destroyed the city if there were fifty righteous people living there (Gen. 18:24-25). And God listened to him, changing the conditions for their preservation five different times. Unfortunately, it wasn't enough.

God is portrayed as an emotional being too. He sees, hears, acts, moves, reacts and responds to his living, moving creation as its living, moving creator.[2] He is a father of the fatherless, and a defender of widows (Ps. 68:5). We see him expressing compassion (Ex. 34:6), and joy (Zeph. 3:17), but also grief and anger—mostly on account of man's sin (Matt. 21:12). In one place he confided in his friend, Samuel, that he regretted having made Saul king over Israel (1 Sam. 15:35).

And God possesses a free will. He chooses and decides things. It was his idea to make man in his likeness. No one was forcing him to do this. He *wanted* to do this. He didn't say, "We *have to* make man," he said, "*Let us* make man." It was all for the sake of love.

AGÁPĒ LOVE

Agápē is the main word used for love in the Bible. The essence of this love relates to how much we appreciate something or someone. "We love the things we value," Winkie Pratney says. It is a love called out of a person's heart by an awakened sense of value in something or someone; a love of approbation and esteem that recognizes the worthiness of the object that is loved.[3]

Agápē love, however, can be misguided. It happens when a person falls in love with the wrong things. We are told that people loved darkness rather than light (John 3:19), and that some loved the praise of men more than the praise of God (John 12:43). John the Evangelist cautioned the church not to fall in love with the world (1 John 2:15), which the Apostle Paul says is what happened to his friend Demas (2 Tim. 4:10). Clearly, agápē love can be used in the wrong way, but it is most powerful when it is used the way it was originally intended.

The deepest and most meaningful relationships are agape-based relationships, because they involve a deep devotion to the person who is the object of our affection. Jesus desired this kind of relationship with Simon Peter when he asked, "Do you love me?" (agapaō). He wanted to know, "Do you love me with the kind of love by which you would be willing to give your life for me one day?" Three times, Peter replied, "Yes, Lord, you know that I am fond (philein) of you" (John 21:15-19). Philein is a friendship built on common tastes and interests. It is very different from agápē love. It wasn't the answer Jesus was hoping for. "He asked for a love of complete devotion. Peter offered him a love of personal heart emotion. He asked for a love of surrendering obedience. Peter offered him a love of personal attachment."[4]

Agápē love does not need to be reciprocated. It can be extended to someone who doesn't love us in return, even, amazingly, to someone who dislikes us. This is why Jesus could say unapologetically that we must love our enemies (Matt. 5:44). But love relationships are different. Love relationships must always involve a mutual exchange. Always! You cannot have a love relationship with someone who doesn't want one with you. It is impossible. Even for God. Relationships can never be one-sided, and therefore, will always include the possibility of rejection.

THE NATURE OF LOVE RELATIONSHIPS

In high school there was a girl I really liked. Her name was Monica. I would have loved to date Monica, but there was a problem. Monica did not find *me* attractive. Consequently, the possibility of a relationship between us was out of the question. It would have been impossible for me to enter into a love relationship with Monica on my own. But what if I was able to make her fall in love with me?

Suppose I possessed the technological knowledge to program a computer chip that could be secretly implanted in Monica's brain while she was sleeping. This chip would cause her to talk and act exactly the way I wanted, although she would think she was choosing it on her own. On one level, it would be the perfect solution to my desire for Monica's affection. Her loving behavior would be everything I wanted. I would, in fact, know exactly what Monica was going to say or do ahead of time. After all, I was the one who programmed her responses.

I'm sure I would have enjoyed such an arrangement for a time, but eventually, I would have grown tired of it. The reason is that deep down, I would know everything Monica was saying or doing, as wonderful as it might be, was really me saying and doing those things to myself. It would be the ultimate act of selfishness on my behalf. Although her actions would seem loving, it wouldn't be love at all. It would all be a sham. There would, in fact, be no real thinking, feeling, or willing person, who was intentionally choosing to love me on her own.

For love to be real, theologian Greg Boyd points out, it must be possible to choose against it. This means that love is, by its very nature, risky. To create a cosmos populated with living beings that are capable of choosing love, required that God create a cosmos in which beings can choose to oppose his will, hurt other people, and damn themselves. If love is the goal, this is the price.[5]

In keeping with this perspective, Evangelist Billy Graham says it is obvious God desired the fellowship of a creature like man. Thus, man was created with a high and exalted purpose, a high and exalted destiny. Man was to be God's closest friend, his partner in the cultivation and development of the earth. He did not create man like a piece of machinery so he could push a button and man would obey him. Man was no robot. Man was a "self." He had dignity and he had ego. He could choose whether he wanted God's friendship and fellowship or not. God did not want his creature to love him because he was forced to do so. This would not be true love. He wanted man's love and fellowship because man chose to love God.[6]

I sometimes come across people who are conflicted over the issue of man's free will. In their minds, this concept clashes with the issue of God's sovereignty. To them, it must be one or the other. Either God is sovereign, or man is free. But why can't it be both? If God is the one who chose to make man free, wasn't that a *sovereign* act on his behalf? Consider this: The idea that man was created with the freedom to accept or reject God's love was one of the core beliefs of the early church fathers. Historian Roger Forster points out that *not a single* leader in the first 300 years of the church rejected the concept of man's free will, and most of them stated it clearly in works that are still in existence today.[7]

THE RIGHT TO CHOOSE

I can pinpoint a handful of decisions that shaped who I am today. Rededicating my life to Christ was the key turning point. Three months later I joined YWAM, got married, and moved to Denver to start a new ministry. All of this happened within the span of seven years. Then the shootings took place, and I was faced with one of the biggest decisions of my life: To become bitter or to choose to forgive. I chose to forgive, and that is what enabled me to move forward in my life.

There is a school of thought that suggests our lives are directed by factors beyond our control, and, therefore, we are not fully responsible for the decisions we make. It's an excuse of course, but it's shocking how many people use it to justify their behavior. It's called determinism. Determinism is the idea that *every* event, including our moral choices, are beyond our control.

Scholar Vishal Mangalwadi observes that determinism implies we don't exist as individual selves but are only products of our chemistry, genes, environment, culture, or language. He describes how his professors in university would couch these ideas in scientific/academic terminology, but it was obvious to him it was no different from the fatalistic worldview he had grown up with in India. "Fatalism," he says, "is a worldview with huge social consequences that I could see all around me: poverty, disease, and oppression. Cultures like mine had historically resigned themselves to their fate."[8]

The truth is, we determine *who* we become. It is not as significant *where* we come from or *what* happens in our lives, as much as *who* we choose to be. Yes, culture, upbringing, and personal experiences are factors, but they are only influences, not a determination.

Matthew Murray grew up in a Christian home with parents who loved him and taught him the ways of God. He received a Christian education from an early age and attended a Bible-believing church his whole life. At some point along the way he got involved in the occult and started experimenting with drugs. His biggest downfall, though, was his unwillingness to forgive the people who hurt him. Ironically, Philip Crouse, who died when Matthew shot him, grew up in a broken home and became a skinhead as a teenager. He was lonely and confused, but had a radical encounter with Jesus Christ that changed the direction of his life. One man had everything going for him and the other nothing, but ultimately, it was the choices they made that determined who they became.

God has always dealt with human beings as free, self-governing entities. He does not coercively control us, to ensure we submit to his will, nor does he lobotomize sinners to make them into saints. God respects our personhood by giving us the freedom to follow him. Or not. Jesus reflected this truth in his story of the prodigal son. It is, perhaps, the clearest example of God's willingness to allow man to go his own way.

The story is one of three parables Jesus told in Luke 15. The first was of a lost sheep, the second of a lost coin, and the third of a lost son. In the first two parables, the owner went searching for what was lost. The shepherd left his flock with a keeper, searching far and wide until he finally found his beloved sheep, carrying it back on his shoulders to the safety of the sheepfold. The owner of the lost coin put aside everything she had planned for the day, sweeping her house, far and wide, until she finally found her precious coin. But in the story of the lost son, the father did not go after his son. Why not? Clearly, he loved him. The reason, I suggest, is because of free will. The sheep was lost *foolishly,* the coin was lost *accidentally,* but the son was lost *by choice!*

The father, although brokenhearted, had to respect his son's freedom to choose his own destiny. If he had tried to force him to return it would only have made things worse for their already strained relationship. The father must have been miserable the whole time his son was away. I'm sure he prayed for him every day and dreamed about him every night. That's what love does to you. Then one day, it happened. I can picture Jesus telling the story to wide-eyed children sitting at his feet by the Sea of Galilee: "But while he was still a long way off," he said, "his father saw him and felt compassion, and ran and embraced him and kissed him" (Luke 15:20).

In his book, *The Autobiography of God,* former U.S. Senate Chaplain Lloyd Ogilvie describes this as the quintessential picture of our heavenly father. It is really a parable of the prodigal God more than the prodigal son, he says. Shocking? Perhaps. But read Jesus' amazing drama again. Then check the definition of prodigal. It means extravagant, lavish, unrestrained. That's the Father's heart for us.

You know exactly how the father felt if you've ever had a wayward son or daughter who finally came home. All you want to do is hold them close, and you are willing to live with whatever mental or emotional baggage they brought back with them. You're just happy they came home. You realize that part of them is still attached to the world, but it doesn't matter. It is like author C. S. Lewis put it: "God will have us," he said, "even though we have shown that we prefer everything else to him and come to him only because there is 'nothing better' now to be had."[9]

Sadly, many prodigals never come home. This was the case with Matthew Murray. At a gathering on the first anniversary of the shootings, his dad stood in front of a packed house of young YWAMers preparing to go on their outreach. "This is what we wanted for our son," he said, fighting back tears. Matthew was their first-born son. They had dreams and ambition for him. They had prayed for him for over twenty years, hoping that one day he would serve God. But he chose a different pathway, and ultimately, there was nothing they could do about it. This is the painful reality God lives with every single moment of every single day.

THE RESULT OF SELFISHNESS

It was only when I lay there on rotting prison straw ... that
I understood that the line separating good and evil passes not
through states, nor between classes, nor between political parties—
but right through every human heart—Alexander Solzhenitsyn

We are facing an unprecedented crisis of inequality in our world today. People living in rich nations, like Germany or the United States, have incomes hundreds of times higher than those living in poor nations, like Mozambique or Honduras. But the problem runs deeper than that, as Solzhenitsyn pointed out. It is a crisis of the human heart. When some take more than they need, others go without. We have, today, the ability to provide food, water, clothing, shelter and health care to *every* human being on earth. Why can't we simply share our resources with others? In one word: Selfishness.

Selfishness is at the heart of all corruption. It is the main reason embezzlement, bribery, and theft happen in business, and why there are still millions of slaves in the world, most of them women and children who are forced to work long hours in unventilated sweatshops. And for what reason? To produce cheap clothing for affluent western nations. Others are trafficked into the perverse world of the sex industry.

Selfishness is the reason we have wars and refugees, and whole families living on garbage dumps in most of the big cities of the developing world. Selfishness has crept into many of the institutions originally designed to help others, like hospitals and care facilities for the aged. And the church is not exempt. Many churches today spend far more on their own comforts and internal programs than on caring for the poor and needy as Jesus commanded.

"It's hard to listen while you preach," U2 singer Bono said in one of his songs.[10] He was right. Selfish people are usually so consumed with their own lives they don't see the negative impact their choices are having on the lives of others. Even their loved ones. Matthew Murray was so fixated on making a statement against injustice he didn't see the pain he was about to cause his own family. Neither did it seem to bother him he was about to take the lives of four innocent people he had never met.

PERSONAL APPLICATION

Even a quick reading of the New Testament makes it clear we have no right to analyze the lives of others until we've analyzed our own. "Let each one test his own work," Paul said (Gal. 6:4). The word "test" here is *dokimazó*, which means, "to examine" or "analyze" one's own self. With this in mind:

Are there things you have said or done that
were really motivated by selfishness?

What was the real reason I said what I said or did what I did? That's the question we must ask ourselves. It doesn't matter what it looks like on the outside, what really matters is the motive of the heart, and if our motive was selfish, we have to make it right, first with God and then with those who were negatively impacted by our selfish words or actions.

Letting the Holy Spirit examine our hearts is the starting point, but we might also need healing from the way others have treated us. Jesus knows the pain we've experienced. He was despised and rejected too (Isa. 53:3). He knows exactly how we feel.

Have you observed the situation from
the other person's perspective?

Something that has helped me tremendously is looking at things from the other person's point of view. This principle is brought forth powerfully in Steven Covey's book, "The 7 Habits of Highly Effective People."

Covey describes an occasion several years ago when he was traveling on a subway in New York City. At one of the stops a man and his children entered the subway car. The children were so loud and rambunctious, yelling back and forth and throwing things. It was very disturbing. And yet, the man did nothing. Covey says it was difficult not to feel irritated. "I could not believe he could be so insensitive as to let his children run wild and do nothing about it, taking no responsibility at all. It was easy to see that everyone else on the subway felt irritated, too." Finally, with what he felt was unusual amount of restraint, he turned to the man and said, "Sir, your children are really disturbing a lot of people. I wonder if you couldn't control them a little more?"

The man lifted his gaze as if to come to an awareness of the situation for the first time and said softly, "Oh, you're right. I guess I should do something about it. We just came from the hospital where their mother died about an hour ago. I don't know what to think, and I guess they don't know how to handle it either."

"Can you imagine what I felt at that moment?" Covey says. "Suddenly I saw things differently, and because I saw things differently, I thought differently, I felt differently, I behaved differently. My irritation vanished. I didn't have to worry about controlling my attitude any longer. My heart was filled with the man's pain. Feelings of sympathy and compassion flowed freely. 'Your wife just died? Oh, I'm so sorry! Can you tell me about it? What can I do to help?' Everything changed in an instant."[11]

Sometimes people act poorly because they are hurting, so seeing things from their vantage point can be extremely helpful. Understanding where they are coming from, then, helps us respond to them out of *their* need, not our own.

Are you willing to forgive those who have hurt you?

Forgiveness is a lot easier to say than to do, of course, but that doesn't lessen its importance. Forgiveness is the key to breaking free from the powerful chains of bitterness and resentment that destroy so many people's lives. This was certainly the case with Matthew Murray. "We raised our son to walk in the ways of God," his mother told me after the shootings, "but he let offenses build up to the point where it was difficult for him to forgive and move on."

What are ways you can get involved in the lives of others?

"Idealism detached from action is just a dream," Bono says, "but idealism allied with pragmatism, with rolling up our sleeves and making the world bend a bit, is very exciting. It's very real. It's very strong." Exactly *what* we do is probably not as important as just *doing something*, but it will always be most fulfilling if we find something we enjoy. If you are good at construction, go build a home for the poor. If you love children, volunteer at a daycare or at your church Sunday School. What skills and talents has God placed within you? Use them to bless others, and the burden will gradually be lifted from your own life.

You might not think you have much to give, but you probably have a lot more to give than you think. The great composer, Beethoven, was like that. He felt inept in social settings. Not only was he an introvert, but he was partially deaf, which made personal conversations difficult. As a result, he would usually keep to himself. But when he heard of the death of a friend's son, Beethoven hurried over to his friend's house. He wasn't sure what to say, but then he saw a piano in the corner of the room. For the next half hour, he played and poured out his emotions in the most expressive way he knew how. When he finished playing, he just got up and left, but his friend remarked later that nobody else's visit had meant so much to him.

CHAPTER THREE

The Fall of Man

Death ends a life, not a relationship.
—MITCH ALBOM

Irma Faulkner was a remarkable woman. She was born into a blue-collar family in the coal mining town of Wollongong, Australia. As a girl, she dreamt of one day becoming a missionary.

After finishing nursing school, she applied to work among the Mengerrdji aboriginal people in Gunbalunya, located in Australia's Northern Territory. After fifteen months there, she returned to Sydney to marry the love of her life, my dad. He had just graduated from Bible college and, like her, had a heart for missions. The Mission Board sent them to Groote Eylandt, a remote island in the Gulf of Carpentaria, and that's where I was born. My mother was the kindest person I have ever known. She truly cared for the needs of others, no matter who they were.

After decades of mission work, mum's health began to fail. First, it was a series of minor strokes, and then, a heart attack. In the end, though, it was cancer that took her life. And just like that, she was gone. She prayed for me on the eve of her death. She was so frail at that point, but her faith was unwavering. She reached over the edge of the bed and placed her feeble hands on top of my head: "Thank you, Lord, for the son you gave to me," she whispered. "Keep your hand on his life and bless him." And then she drifted off to sleep again. I will never cease thanking God for my mother. She prayed for my sisters and me every day of her life. But why did such a loving, godly person have to go like that, and why did she suffer so much at the end?

GOD'S PLAN A

Many people wrestle with suffering and death issues like this, including our own community after the shootings. Ultimately, we found solace in the creation story. It was clear to us that God never intended for death to be part of his beautiful created world. His plan was always for man to live forever, and, as far as we could tell from scripture, he intended for this to take place on earth.

It is possible God had been developing the "animal" form of man for many centuries before it was finally "perfected" and ready to become the vessel of humanity and the image of himself. He gave it hands whose thumb could be applied to each of the fingers, and jaws and teeth, and a throat capable of articulation, and a brain sufficiently complex to execute all the material motions whereby rational thought is incarnated. The creature may have existed for ages in this state before it became man. It may even have been clever enough to make things, which a modern archeologist would accept as proof of its humanity. But it was still only an animal because all its physical processes were directed to purely material and natural ends.

Then, in the fullness of time, God caused to descend upon this organism, both on its psychology and its physiology, a new kind of consciousness which could say "I" and "me," which could look upon itself as an object, which knew God, which could make judgments of truth, beauty and goodness, and which was so far above time that it could perceive time flowing past.[1]

God's plan was to make man a partner with him in the development and management of the earth (Gen. 1:28). He breathed into his nostrils the breath of life, and man became a living being (Gen. 2:7). In that instant, the creature went from being a hollow shell, to becoming a real person, with a living spirit, and a personality resembling God himself. He now possessed the capacity to dream, to feel, to think, and to love—but also, to hate, to be self-centered, and to oppose God.

But sin was never part of the original plan. God never wanted for man to turn against him, and then suffer the horrible consequences of that decision: Banishment from the Garden of Eden and eventual death (Rom. 6:23). Up until that moment the dream was still alive—the dream of a future partnership, with no death or mourning or crying or pain. It was the dream that had prompted God to exclaim on the sixth day of creation, that everything he had made was good (Gen. 1:31).

Following God's creation of man, he built around him a perfect environment conducive to life on earth, with fountains that sprang up from the ground and animals that roamed freely with no fear of men. He planted trees filled with nourishing and delicious fruit, and weeds and thorn bushes were nowhere to be found in God's garden (Gen. 2:5-19). It was the perfect ecosystem designed by the ultimate landscape architect.

And that wasn't even the best part. Sickness and death were also nonexistent, because God had planted a tree in the middle of his garden called the tree of life. Eating from this tree, then, would keep man from the decrepitude of age that ends in death. As soon as he started to feel ill, all man would have to do was eat from the tree of life and all infection or cancer would instantly be eradicated from his body. Its life-giving properties would counteract the effects of wear and tear on his animal frame, so that his life would literally never come to an end. That was *plan A*. God's original intent was for us to live forever, in perfect harmony with himself and the rest of his creation. But then came The Fall.

PARADISE LOST

There was another tree in God's garden, but this one was off-limits to man. It was a tree that came with a solemn warning: *"Of the tree of the knowledge of good and evil you shall not eat, for in the day that you eat of it you shall surely die"* (Gen. 2:17). If man ate from this tree he would replace God as the final authority in his life. Instead of God, man would now be calling the shots. He would be in charge. He, not God, would decide what was good and evil in the world.

We can see evidences of man's decision to replace God everywhere we look—in government, education, and the judicial system. Even in the way parents raise their children. Man has become convinced his way is better than God's. In some cases, we have drifted so far from God's standards we have now begun calling wrong things right and right things wrong. And God simply responds, "There is a way that seems right to a man, but its end is the way to death" (Prov. 14:12).

But let's back up for a moment. Why would a loving God put such a dangerous tree in the garden to begin with? Wouldn't it have been better if he had created an environment completely devoid of temptation and the possibility of sin? God could have prevented The Fall if he had never created such a forbidden tree. The trouble with that is that love must always have an option. Only a free being with an independent will can love. As Roger Forster points out, "If love was to be a meaningful thing, Adam had to be allowed some form of free choice. God allowed him the freedom to choose wrongly, but nothing indicates he wanted him to do so."[2]

THE DOMINO EFFECT

Our decision to disobey God is the greatest tragedy in human history, because that *one* decision radically impacted the life of every human being who was yet to be born on earth. In one fell swoop, death came to the entire human race. God separated man from the tree of life, and from that point onward, man became a mortal. We have a nicer way of saying it of course, it is called "aging." But the reality is aging is simply the power of death gradually taking over until it finally wins the war.

Romans 5:12 describes the domino effect of sin like this: "… sin entered the world through one man, and death through (his) sin, and (this) death has spread to all mankind …" Like a degenerative disease, death will eventually take the life of every person on earth. Are there exceptions? Yes. Two of them we know about: Enoch, who was "taken up so that he should not see death" (Heb. 11:5), and Elijah, who "went up by a whirlwind into heaven" (2 Kings 2:11). But unless God decides to make another exception, the rest of us are going to die.

THE SENTENCE GOD NEVER FINISHED

This raises an interesting question. Was it really necessary for God to separate man from the one thing that was giving him life? After all, God never wanted man to die in the fist place. Why not let him live on despite his sin? We find the answer to this question in a dialogue between the Father, Son, and Holy Spirit. In this conversation God is reflecting on what has just taken place—man has eaten from the tree of the knowledge of good and evil, but the tree of life is still within his grasp. This meant he still had the ability to live forever, but now, in a corrupt, fallen state. Suddenly, mid-sentence, God stops what he is saying, and immediately begins the process of removing man from the garden.

The passage is shocking when you first read it: "Behold, the man has become like one of us, knowing good and evil. And now, lest he reach out his hand and take also from the tree of life, and eat, and live forever ..." (Gen. 3:22 BSB). The verse literally ends without God finishing what he had begun to say. The thought of man living forever, but now in his fallen state, must have been so horrible that God felt he needed to act immediately, and put as much distance as possible between man and the tree of life.

Think about it for a moment. Can you imagine a world in which evil people lived forever? What would life on earth be like if ruthless men like Ivan the Terrible or Adolf Hitler were immortal? Billy Graham speculated that if God had not imposed physical death on humankind, men would have continued in their sin until eventually the entire earth would have become hell itself.[3] Can anyone blame God for taking such drastic measures?

THE FLOOD

There was another worldwide event that dramatically impacted the physical wellbeing of humanity: The Flood. Leading up to this event there was, living on earth, a mutant life form born from the unnatural sexual union between fallen angels and women (Gen. 6:2). They were a kind of part-angel part-human hybrid species called "The Nephilim" (Gen. 6:4). This mutant race of quasi-people was corrupting the human gene pool and disrupting God's creative order in which everything was intended to reproduce according to its own kind (Gen. 1:21-25). It was, in a sense, sabotaging God's original plan to populate the earth with beings made in his own image (Gen. 1:26), and this "grieved him to his heart" (Gen. 6:6). So much so that he decided to start over again.

The aftereffects of the great deluge can be seen throughout the earth today. Although some have speculated that millions of years of water flow must be responsible for the erosion of the top layer of the earth, geologists are now telling us a sizable amount of water in a much shorter period could have produced the same geological effect. But the greatest impact was on man, whose life span shortened with each successive generation. Whereas people had been living 700, 800, and even 900 years prior to the flood, just a few generations following, man was now living barely past 100.[4] All this helps us understand the reason we die, but why does pain have to be part of the equation?

THE GIFT OF PAIN

How singular is this thing called pleasure and how curiously related to pain, which might be thought to be the opposite ... yet he who pursues either is generally compelled to take the other—Socrates

In their book, *The Gift of Pain*, Philip Yancey and Dr. Paul Brand raise an interesting question. What would a world without pain be like, and could such a place exist? It actually does exist, but it is no utopia. It is a colony for leprosy patients, a world where people literally feel no pain, and reap the horrifying consequences. During his work with leprosy patients in India, Dr. Brand became convinced pain truly is one of God's great gifts to mankind. He points out it is the primary indicator that tells us something is wrong. Pain has a value that becomes clearest in its absence. It is the gift nobody wants, yet the gift none of us can do without."[5]

"At one end of the spectrum we have pleasure, and at the other, a warning system that alerts our brains that something is wrong," author Mike Saia explains. We probably can't have one without the other. "A person can place his cold hands close to a fire, and experience the pleasure of warmth, but if he puts them too close, he will experience the pain of burning. The stimulus, warmth and burning, is the same in both cases. It's the degree of the stimulus that produces either pleasure or pain."[6]

Closely associated with physical suffering is the problem of mental and emotional suffering. In his book, *The Problem of Pain*, C.S. Lewis raises the subject of man's God-given ability to reason, whereby he is enabled to foresee his own death. This knowledge brings him acute mental suffering due to his inherent desire for permanence.[7] Awareness of his mortality, then, can give rise to fear and depression. This is a challenge some have addressed through the use of chemicals, but there is a better way. Amid a broken world God offers us a sound mind. The word that expresses this in the New Testament is, *"sóphronizó,"* which can be translated, "self-discipline," or "self-control," but also means, "a sound mind" (2 Tim. 1:7). And to those terrified by the finality of their existence, God offers hope, that if they believe in him, they will never die, but have everlasting life (John 3:16).

THE MYSTERY OF HEALING

Except for the final generation alive on earth when Christ returns, the rest of us are all going to die. Yet, along the way, God heals some of us. He heals some but not others. It is still a mystery to me. And if we look to the scriptures for understanding we are likely to come away frustrated because there is no clear explanation. Faith and prayer have something to do with it, but not always. It is an oversimplification to think a person will always be healed if they have faith. Nonetheless, God *does* heal people, and there are thousands of examples to prove it. One of them is our daughter, Rachel.

She had been leading a YWAM outreach in California following the shootings. While her team was staying at a ranch, she and a friend decided to go horseback riding. The ride went well, until they headed back. Without warning, Rachel's horse took off at a full gallop. Nearing the ranch's front gate, her horse jerked to a stop, throwing Rachel head-first onto the gravel road. She lay there motionless for a few moments until her team came running to help.

At the same time Linda and I were back in Denver, meeting with, of all people, the parents of Matthew Murray. They had asked to visit the place where the shootings had taken place, hoping to get some closure to the nightmare they had been living with for the previous six weeks. I took them to the hallway where everything had happened. Several of the bullet marks were still visible on the wall, and they wept as the memory of that night flooded over them once again. Then we came back to our house for a time of prayer. That is when we got the call.

It was one of the students calling my wife's cell phone as they were loading Rachel onto an ambulance. We could hear Linda asking, "Can she move her hands and feet?" "Is she able to talk?" "Can you put one of the paramedics on the phone?" But none of the paramedics would talk to us because of a U.S. law preventing them from disclosing health information without a patient's consent or knowledge. There seemed to be no way to get clarity on Rachel's condition, except for what can only be described as the divine intervention of God. Very few people could have helped us at that moment, but Dr. Ron Murray was one of them.

As a neurologist Ron was able to call another specialist in California, and within a few minutes had all the information we needed. "You guys need to get out there right away," he said, "this is very serious." Four hours later we were on a plane to Fresno. When we got to the hospital Rachel lay somewhat motionless, still unwashed and bloodied from the accident. She had twenty-four fractures in her skull and jawbone. A few days later she developed a paralysis on the left side of her face from the nerve injury. It is hard to put into words how difficult it was for us as parents.

In the coming days, people all around the world prayed for Rachel, and miraculously, God restored her. All 24 fractures healed, and the paralysis disappeared. Everything came back to normal except her sense of smell. She lived without full olfactory function for the next 18 months, and then, the second part of the healing took place. Stefaan Hugo, a visiting YWAM leader from South Africa, set aside an evening to pray for the sick. Someone said, "Hey, why don't we have him to pray for Rachel?" But Stefaan was busy praying for others, so they grabbed one of the guys on his team.

This large tattooed man looked more like a nightclub bouncer than a preacher, but he approached Rachel and began to pray. When he opened his eyes, he said something no one could have predicted. "God told me to put my fingers up your nose," he said. And with that he stuck his right index and middle fingers in Rachel's nose. Immediately she could smell again.

As incredible as this story is, there are just as many examples of people who were never healed. It is a mystery none of us can fully explain, but the point we cannot afford to miss is that God's healing has nothing to do with his love for us. He loves the *whole* world (John 3:16). It's important to factor in also, that even when a person is healed, their healing is only temporary. Every one of us, including those who have experienced God's healing touch, are still going to die. The weight of sin is simply too great for any of us to bear. Eventually, sin is going to win the fight, that is, until we get the ultimate upgrade. Before we discuss that, however, there is one other element in this picture that bears mentioning.

REAPING WHAT OTHERS HAVE SOWN

How is it fair that we inherited this tendency to sin, with all its negative consequences, as a result of choices made thousands of years before any of us were born? If you ever wondered that, you are right. It is not fair, which is why God made a way, through Christ, to give us a second chance (1 Cor. 15:22). It is why he is called the second (or last) Adam (1 Cor. 15:45). Through him, we can have eternal life once again. This fact, in and of itself, speaks to the justice of God. It is his way of saying, "Okay, I know you got a raw deal through what Adam and Eve did, so I am going to make it up to you by giving you a second chance."

This second chance will include brand new bodies impervious to sin, pain, and death. Until then, however, we must live in these less-than-perfect ones, sharing the planet with millions of less-than-perfect people, who, like Adam and Eve, have the capacity to perpetuate suffering through their poor choices. A mother who smokes or drinks alcohol during pregnancy will negatively impact the physical wellbeing of her unborn baby. Parents who get a divorce have a negative impact on the lives of their children. The children did nothing wrong, yet they reap the consequences of their parents' decisions. In a similar way, Adam and Eve's decision to disobey God had a negative impact on all future generations yet to be born on earth.

EDEN RESTORED

So he passed over, and all the trumpets sounded
for him on the other side—John Bunyan

There is a deep yearning in the heart of every man and woman for restoration. We know intuitively something has gone terribly wrong in our world and we desperately long to see it made right again. In her epic song, *Woodstock*, Joni Mitchell recounts the story of that legendary music festival where masses of flower children and curious onlookers gathered on a dairy farm in upstate New York for three days of peace and music. The year was 1969.

It was the gathering of the century, and in the minds of many, the beginning of a countercultural revolution that is still playing itself out in American society today. *"We are stardust; we are golden, we are a billion-year-old carbon, and we've got to get ourselves back to the garden"* she wrote.[8] Not entirely true in terms of the origin of our species, but her lyrics struck a chord deep within the heart of a generation ripped apart by the Vietnam War, and the assassinations of Martin Luther King Jr. and the Kennedys. It put words to a desperate longing to recapture a paradise lost. And on the other side of the Atlantic, John and Yoko were echoing the same sentiment. "All we are saying is give peace a chance," they implored.[9] Their vision of utopia, however, was never going to happen without God, which is why the garden was always out of reach—but not forever.

The story of the Bible, from Genesis to Revelation, is the story of God's desire to restore this broken world, and one day we will see it with our own eyes. "The Bible begins and ends with the same scene: Paradise, a river, the luminous glory of God, and the tree of life. All of human history takes place somewhere between the first part of Genesis and the last part of Revelation, and everything in between comprises man's struggle to regain what was lost."[10]

And it *will be* regained. God didn't actually destroy the tree of life. He just moved it to a new location. We will join the saints of history as citizens of a brand new city whose architect and builder is God (Heb. 11:6). Our appearance will probably resemble the bodies we were originally meant to have before The Fall. There will be no arthritis, cancer, or heart disease. There will be no more death or mourning or crying or pain. We will be perfect in every way, restored to God's original design.

"Everything in respect to heaven will be new," Billy Graham observed. "... The paradise that man lost will be regained, but it will be much more. It will be a new paradise, not the old one repaired and made over. When God says, 'Behold, I make all things new,' (Rev. 21:5) the emphasis is on 'all things.' We are going to live in a brand-new world."[11]

When we get there, we will finally be home. It is a place we have never seen before, but it will feel like home because it is the place where we were always intended to live. Yes, death will have left its mark, as Charles Dickens observed, "a void so wide and deep that nothing but the width and depth of eternity can fill up" ... and it *will* be filled up. The Bible promises that in that moment, death will be "swallowed up in victory" (1 Cor. 15:54).

This is why the Bible can unapologetically declare that the sufferings of the present time are not worthy to be compared with everything God has in store for us (Rom. 8:18).

No one can be blamed, though, for wanting to stay here on earth, but it is only because of our fear of the unknown. Nothing in our present existence could prepare us for the glorious life ahead. The closest comparison is one none of us can remember, because it happened the day we were born. Up until that point, your whole world is warm, safe, and secure. Then one day you feel a tug. The walls around you begin to press in and you are being pulled through a tunnel. You see a piercing, blinding light. Cold, rough hands reach in and begin to pull you through the tunnel and hold you upside down. Then there's a painful slap. Waaahhhh! Congratulations, you have just been born.

"Death is like that," Philip Yancey says. "On this end of the birth canal, it's a scary dark tunnel, and you are being sucked by an irresistible force. None of us looks forward to it. We're afraid. It's full of pressure, pain, darkness ... the unknown. But beyond the darkness and the pain lies a whole new world. When we awaken after death in that bright new world, our tears and hurts will be mere memories."[12]

All this, of course, was only made possible by the cross. "Jesus' resurrection and victory over death brought a decisive new word to the vocabulary of pain and suffering: Temporary! Jesus Christ holds out the startling promise of an afterlife without pain. Whatever anguish we feel now will not last."[13] No death, no sorrow, no crying, no pain. That is what we can look forward to (Rev. 21:4). "We have only shadow notions of that future state now. We are locked in a dark room, like the setting of Sartre's play, *No Exit*. But chinks of light are seeping through—virtue, glory, beauty, compassion, hints of truth and justice—suggesting that beyond those walls, there exists another world."[14]

PERSONAL APPLICATION

How have sickness and death impacted your relationship with God?

Yancey pictures a scenario in which vandals break into a museum displaying works from Picasso's Blue Period. Motivated by sheer destructiveness, they splash red paint all over the paintings and slash them with knives. It would be the height of unfairness, if someone were to display these works as representative of the artist. The same applies to God's creation. This was not what he wanted for the human race! "God has already hung a 'condemned' sign above the earth, and has promised judgment and restoration. That this world, spoiled by evil and suffering, still exists at all is an example of God's mercy, not his cruelty."[15]

The sickness and death we see in the world are not God's doing. We are the ones at fault and he is more brokenhearted than we are at the way things turned out. Once we recognize this fact, everything else begins to make sense, but we still have to deal with the raw emotions of our own suffering. If you have blamed God for the loss of a loved one, a diagnosis of cancer, a tragic accident or some unspeakable crime, you need to release him from that charge. Tell him you no longer hold him responsible for what took place, and affirm that he loves you and you love him.

Have you prayed for someone's healing without seeing significant results? How has that affected you?

John Wimber tells of a time when he was pastoring one of the first Vineyard churches in California. One day God told him to begin praying for the sick. "It was one of the most miserable times in my life," he recalls. "Not one person was healed in a period of about ten months. And to make things worse, people started leaving the church. They were upset by what I was teaching. I wasn't sure myself." But God just kept driving him back to the passages in Luke where Jesus healed the sick.

Wimber tried to teach out of a different book of the Bible. He even tried to quit teaching altogether. One day God spoke to him rather sternly, "Either teach my Word or get out." Get out? Get out of what? The ministry? The book? What? Don't let your experience compromise my Word," the Lord spoke to him. Suddenly he saw that he was letting his lack of success control what the scripture said and it broke his heart. "I got on my knees and repented," he said, "and shortly thereafter we saw our first healing."

So what about you? Has your lack of success kept you from praying for the sick? In Hebrews the point is clear: We cannot quit simply because we haven't seen results. "For you have need of endurance," it says, "so that when you have done the will of God you may receive what is promised" (Heb 10:36).

What are you doing to take care of your body?

Sometimes we expect to live long and healthy lives without taking care of ourselves. Nutrition and exercise are *our* responsibility. Like a car that requires regular maintenance, our bodies were designed to be serviced on a regular basis. Even small measures can make a big difference in the long run, like eating a healthy breakfast, or regularly taking walks. If you need to take this responsibility more seriously, just start by implementing small habits and you'll put yourself in the best position to live a long and healthy life.

CHAPTER FOUR

The decay of the earth

*If this is the best of all possible worlds, then
what are the others like?*

—VOLTAIRE

From outer space there are fewer sights more peaceful than our green and blue planet with white puffy clouds slowly meandering across the continents. Get a little closer, though, and you begin to realize things are not as peaceful as they seem. Earthquakes, volcanoes, and violent storms are regular occurrences, let alone floods, wildfires, and now, rising sea levels. And the poorest of the poor are most at risk. The people of Haiti, Bangladesh, and Indonesia have all experienced suffering in multiple natural disasters, and many have no doubt wondered what they did to deserve such cruel punishment. Didn't God say everything was good when he first created the earth? (Gen. 1:31). It sure does not seem that way now.

EVALUATING THE FACTS

Natural disasters are a sad reality in the world in which we live, impacting millions of people every year. We call them "natural" because they come from a natural, rather than a human source. They are sometimes related to weather, geology, biology or even factors outside the earth's atmosphere, but they almost always result in large-scale loss of life or damage to property.

On Christmas 2004, I flipped open my laptop one last time before going to bed and saw breaking news of an earthquake off the coast of Sumatra, Indonesia. "They're saying it was 9.3 on the Richter scale," I said to my wife who was sitting in the other room. "That is one huge earthquake!" And it was. It turned out to be the third largest earthquake in recorded history, and the longest in terms of duration. Its shaking was so violent it caused the earth to vibrate back and forth as much as 1 cm (0.4 inches). Over the next few days, we watched in horror as images of 100-foot waves crashed against coastal communities in Southeast Asia and the Indian subcontinent. It was sickening. Almost a quarter of a million people lost their lives.

About forty earthquakes in history have measured 8.5 or higher on the Moment Magnitude Scale (MMS), and half a dozen of those have eclipsed the 9.0 mark, including the one that caused the Indian Ocean tsunamis in 2004. The largest earthquake ever recorded shook the town of Valdivia, Chile in 1960, measuring 9.5 and triggering 80-foot tsunamis that raced across the Pacific Ocean, devastating coastal villages in Hawaii, Japan, and the Philippines.

According to researchers at the Seismological Society of America, computer models of future seismic activity suggest the Pacific earthquake zone should only be capable of generating shocks of magnitude 9.0 or higher every 10,000 years. Therefore, it came as a complete surprise when there was a 9.3

earthquake just 44 years after Valdivia, and then, a 9.1 off the coast of Japan seven years after that. What is going on? They resemble the contractions of a woman in labor, growing in frequency and intensity, until the moment of birth. And maybe that is exactly what they are—contractions leading up to the final moment of Christ's return to earth (Matt. 24:8).

HYDROLOGICAL DISASTERS

Water is to blame for most of the world's worst natural disasters. We desperately need this precious resource, but too much or too little of it can result in devastating environmental damage. Hailstorms, cyclones, tornadoes, and floods are all considered hydrological disasters. But so are droughts. A drought can last for months, and even years, causing crop failure, and leaving vast areas vulnerable to dust storms and fire.

This was the case during the 1930s Dust Bowl in the United States, which extended across 100 million acres in Colorado, Texas, and the Midwest. The worst drought since 2000 happened in northeast Africa in 2011. It affected 12 million people in Kenya, Somalia, Ethiopia, and Djibouti, and over 200,000 lost their lives. Tragically, half of them were children under the age of five. Drought is now afflicting millions more throughout the Sahel region of Africa, and in Canada and Australia, a lack of rain is sparking an unprecedented number of forest fires.

The deadliest hydrological disaster was a flood in China in 1931, which took the lives of 4 million people.[1] It, too, began with a protracted period of drought during the late 1920s. This was followed by heavy mountain snowstorms the following winter, and, when the spring thaw arrived it coincided with heavy rains, including nine separate cyclones (up from the usual two). The result was catastrophic. An unprecedented buildup of water flooded the Yangtze, Huai, and Yellow Rivers.

An estimated 53 million were left homeless, and many flood victims died from starvation and waterborne diseases like cholera and typhus in the weeks and months that followed.

Of course, the greatest natural disaster in history was also a flood. Fortunately, God promised he would never allow that to happen again (Gen. 9:11). Keep in mind that prior to the Great Flood, there was no precipitation in the form of rain, so no one ever perished in an avalanche, or drowned in a violent storm, or starved because their crops were decimated by hail. Instead of precipitation, the earth was watered by springs that bubbled up from the ground (Gen. 2:6), and there was a protective layer above the earth separating the waters above and the waters below, like a gigantic greenhouse in which man could thrive (Gen. 1:7). But when the flood came, the canopy over the earth collapsed, opening the door for rainstorms, cyclones, and other forms of extreme weather to become commonplace, let alone an increase in harmful radiation from the sun.

VOLCANOES

Another force that is shaping and reshaping the earth is volcanism. Volcanoes are found on every continent, and their destructive force is terrifying. When the south Asian island of Krakatoa exploded in 1883, the blast was heard 3,000 miles away, and it created a 150-foot-tall tsunami that shot across the Indian Ocean at 500 miles an hour.

The world's most active volcano is Mount Kilauea, which has been spewing lava since 1983 on Hawaii's Big Island. On most days though, Kilauea just percolates along, venting sulfur dioxide and gurgling magma to the delight of the tourists who visit Hawaii's Volcanoes National Park. On rare occasions, this usually docile mountain will overflow, torching the homes of those who live nearby.

This is what happened to my friends Marty and Mindy Berry. Their story is so surreal it almost seems made up. Unfortunately, it is not. In early 2018 they moved into their dream home on Kapoho Bay, considered by many to be the most picturesque place in all of the Hawaiian Islands—a tropical paradise, with warm hot springs, natural tide-pools and black sandy beaches—but not any more.

On April 9th, 2018 the Berrys closed escrow on their new house, but the timing couldn't have been worse. Less than one month later, Kilauea began erupting along the lower east rift zone, about ten miles from the Berrys' home. "On May 29th, our electricity and cell phone coverage went out," Mindy told me. "Hawaii Civil Defense didn't expect the lava would ever reach Kapoho, but they advised us to take our essential belongings and leave town until the road and power could be repaired.

"That was the last time we saw our home. Less than a week later, what was once the most beautiful place in Hawaii, vanished from the face of the earth. It is as though it was never even there," Mindy said.[2]

Kilauea's ten eruptions to date are tame compared to other blasts that have terrorized our planet. You have probably heard the names: Vesuvius, Etna, Pinatubo, and Mount St. Helens, to name a few. All left their mark on the earth and the lives of those living close by. The largest eruption in the last several centuries was Mount Tambora in Indonesia. The explosion is thought to be responsible for lowering global temperatures by at least five degrees Fahrenheit in the places where the cloud of ash obscured the sun. The result was "the year without summer." Crops failed, livestock perished, and a foot of snow fell in Quebec City, Canada in the middle of summer 1816. The blast is also credited with the invention of the bicycle, due to the death of so many horses. Natural disasters are a sad reality in the world in which we live, and more than a few have wondered why a God of love would create a planet with so many vulnerabilities. This is the explanation the Bible puts forth:

THE DOWNWARD SPIRAL OF THE EARTH

The earth has been in a gradual state of decline for thousands of years. Much like our physical bodies, our planet is dying too. We are not evolving as they told us—the exact opposite is true. The disintegration of matter and energy in the universe is headed toward an ultimate state of inertia unless, of course, God intervenes.

For 150 years, the so-called experts have been telling us everything came from nothing. They are fools for believing such a lie. The truth is a loving creator fashioned the perfect environment conducive to life and happiness in the midst of his vast universe (Gen. 1:1). But then sin entered the world and it disrupted everything.

As the righteous judge of his created world, God could not stand by and pretend like nothing had happened. If he had done so, he would be violating the integrity of his own character. His commitment to righteousness compels him to show mercy only when the conditions of justice have also been met. One might say, "but he is God. He can do anything he wants." True, *physically* he can, but he is also the *moral* ruler of his universe, and, as such, he is committed to doing what is just and right in every situation.

When it came to the human race, God felt the severity of our transgression required an appropriate response. This was not a small matter. He could have wiped us out altogether, and been fully justified in doing so. Instead, he cursed the ground (Gen. 3:17). Immediately, the planet was thrust into a downward spiral of chaos and disarray (Rom. 8:20). The harmony that once existed in the cosmos was compromised, and creation stopped responding to man's efforts as it had before. Adam would now have to sweat and toil to make a living, and weeds and thorn bushes would flourish where beautiful gardens once stood (Gen. 3:18). That is where we are today. We only have ourselves to blame.

Let's also note that God's motivation in cursing the ground was not unloving. It might seem that way on the surface, but consider this: When humans have an abundance of spare time, they tend to use it for their own selfish purposes, that is, they sin. Or to put it another way, there was a redemptive purpose within God's seemingly harsh reaction. Mike Saia reasons that God purposely made it more difficult for man to get food from the ground so he would have less free time to sin.[3]

All of this was compounded by the growth of briars and thorn bushes, plants that had not existed previously, or at least not in that same form. It is difficult to tell from the wording in Genesis if this was an intended part of the curse, or simply a consequence, but either way, more briars and thorn bushes meant more difficult farming, and less time for leisure and selfishness. There was also a limitation of edible plants, since every green plant could be eaten prior to the curse (Gen. 1:29), but were now inedible or poisonous.

A RAPIDLY AGING PLANET

Do you remember your first car? For most of us it was a hand-me-down with many thousands of miles on the odometer. If it was anything like mine, blue smoke was coming from the exhaust pipe, and the alternator light would come on every time I went up a hill. If I hadn't treated her with a lot of TLC, she would have fallen apart a lot sooner than she finally did.

Our rapidly aging planet is like this. We are fast approaching terminal velocity in our race toward extinction. Many of our unwise choices—deforestation, water pollution, and the use of chemical fertilizers—are literally choking our planet to death. Meanwhile, trash has been building up in the world's oceans. A recent study discovered plastic pollution in the world's oceans has been "increasing exponentially" since measurements began in 1970. Almost 80,000 metric tons of plastic have built up in an area referred to as "The Great Pacific Garbage Patch," between California and Hawaii. It is now twice the size of Texas.

The primary culprit for the decay of our planet, however, is not carelessness, but sin. Earthquakes, volcanoes, and hurricanes are the reflection of our decision to turn away from God. The *fait accompli* of our poor choices has not only affected our physical bodies, it is also killing this once-pristine habitat we call home.

PERSONAL APPLICATION

We are all responsible—Pope Francis

What practical steps are you taking to steward God's creation?

The first responsibility God gave to man was to manage the earth and everything that dwells within it (Gen. 1:28). No one else is going to do this if we don't. Getting everyone to work together, however, is a challenge, especially when large corporations and nation-states have much to gain by cutting corners. Even so, each of us must do our part to curb the pollution and disease that has come from our past carelessness.

With natural disasters happening all across the planet, are there ways you can help in your area or some other part of your nation or the world?

Our compassionate God does not want us to sit by idly while it's in our power to help alleviate the suffering of our neighbors, whether they live in our community or in another country. The next time you hear of a natural disaster, ask God how you can be involved. We in YWAM have discovered that people who have suffered great loss are often more open to God when they are touched by the kindness of his people.

Whole books have been written on the subject of the decay of the earth, but what is almost always overlooked is the impact of *our morality* on the environment. This is much more than just a physical thing. God says in his Word that if his people will turn from their wicked ways he will "heal their land" (2 Chron. 7:14). Can this really be what God meant to imply? That living a godly life has a direct impact on the physical environment? There seems to be no other way to accurately interpret this passage, especially when we consider that his promise of restoration came during a time of drought and famine in the land (2 Chron. 7:13).

The ultimate healing, of course, will not come until the Messiah returns to set up his Kingdom on earth. That will be the occasion of God's final restoration, when the curse that has crippled creation will finally be lifted, and everything will revert back to its original state (Rev. 22:3). The age will be unlike anything the world has ever known. The Kingdom of God will triumph. The scripture says, "But we are looking forward to the new heavens and new earth he has promised, a world filled with God's righteousness" (2 Pet. 3:13 NLT).

In what ways are you living with an eternal perspective in mind?

God calls us to live our lives in the light of eternity, not drawing our comfort and security from the things we see but from the things we cannot see. It's because the things we see are transient, but the things we cannot see are eternal (2 Cor. 4:18). My friends Marty and Mindy Berry chose to live this way. They did not blame God for their horrendous circumstances, but responded like Job (Job 1:20). When the news came that their home had been destroyed by the lava flow, they got on their knees and worshipped.

> "It's a holy place of surrender that we live in now," Mindy told me. "Our love for God goes far beyond what this world has to offer. Marty and I are still rich in what matters most—love. It is so simple yet so profound. We've been living out of suitcases for over six months. Weary? Yes. Heartbroken? Yes. Do we know the future? No. But we trust the one who holds the future, and in that we have peace."[4]

CHAPTER FIVE

Ignorance

Acquire wisdom, and with all your acquiring, get understanding.

—KING SOLOMON

French Nobel Prize winner Albert Camus said he believed much of the evil in the world came from ignorance, and good intentions could do just as much harm as malevolence if they lacked understanding. He was right. Good intentions do not guarantee a good outcome.

Usually naïve people are not out to hurt anyone, but a lack of understanding leads them to make decisions that are harmful to themselves or others. Are they responsible for their actions? It depends. If their ignorance stems from laziness or a failure to be informed about something they *should have known*, then yes, they are responsible for the outcome. But sometimes the outcome of a decision is beyond a person's ability to know. Let's look at these two categories: Ignorance stemming from a failure to be informed, and ignorance stemming from a lack of information.

NEGLIGENCE

One of our teams barely escaped a negligence-based trag-edy during an outreach to Anchorage, Alaska several years ago. They were invited to dinner at the house of a man they had met at church. The host was an avid hunter with a collection of rifles and animal trophies, and he was eager to show them off. The man pointed to a musket hanging on the wall. "I made that one myself," he said.

John Murphy, one of the young men on our team, told me, "We were admiring the guy's work of art, passing the musket around and even looking down the barrel. Then one of the staff guys took it inside to show the girls who were sitting in the living room. He sat on the couch, pointed the rifle at the ground, and then, cocked the hammer and pulled the trigger."

"It went off with the loudest bang you have ever heard," John said. "Why this guy had a loaded gun hanging on his wall beats me, but he did. The musket ball shattered on the concrete floor, and shrapnel and pieces of concrete went flying through-out the room. When the smoke cleared, only one of us had been hit. One of our Norwegian students had a drop of blood trickling down his neck, but he was fine. It turned out to be a gunpowder-burn from the gun going off right next to him. But things could have been much, much worse," John confessed.

Some negligent decisions or indecisions have much greater consequences. The D-Day invasion on June 6, 1944 has long been considered a turning point in World War II. But just five weeks before to the invasion, a beach landing rehearsal called Operation Tiger resulted in the deaths of nearly 1,000 U.S. troops in the south of England. Landing craft carrying tanks and troops were easy prey for Nazi submarines that attacked the rear of the convoy. According to the BBC, a series of tragic decisions, including the unexpected removal of a British Navy destroyer escort and failure to coordinate radio frequencies, led to the loss of three ships. Many men died of drowning and hypothermia because of incorrectly worn lifejackets. The tragedy, which was kept secret for decades, sparked strategic improvements that helped the D-Day invaders. But these changes came at a great price.

King Solomon was right. Even if it comes at a great cost, we have to find a way to acquire understanding before making important decisions (Prov. 4:7). Wisdom and understanding are crucial to preempting negligence-based suffering. The same is true of our words. Negligent speech is the source of much suffering in our world. James describes them as rudders that can change the direction of an entire ship (James 3:4). How many relationships have been damaged or destroyed because of a failure to use wisdom in the way we speak? And God does not take our words lightly. Jesus said when we stand before him one day, we will be asked to give an account for *every* careless word we have spoken (Matt. 12:36).

INNOCENCE

Ignorance is not an excuse if we *should have known* better, but sometimes the outcome of a decision is beyond our ability to know, yet, with equally devastating consequences. Take cigarette smoking in the last century for example.

Millions of men and women began smoking during World War II. By the mid 1940's, cigarette production had surpassed 300 billion a year, and no one thought twice about it until 1964 when the U.S. Surgeon General wrote a scathing report on the dangers of cigarette smoking. His paper concluded the nicotine and tar in cigarettes was the primary reason so many people were dying from heart disease and lung cancer.

Many stopped smoking immediately, but others ignored the warning. That was when they crossed the line from *innocence* to *negligence*. But hey, it was their constitutional right to do whatever they pleased with their bodies, right? In retrospect, it turned out to be much more than a personal decision because of the enormous strain it put on the healthcare system and on the lives of those inhaling their secondhand smoke. In my home country of Australia, the government has tried to curb the problem by printing graphic photos of cancer-ridden patients on cigarette packs and imposing astronomical taxes on tobacco products, Unfortunately, many still smoke, especially young adults.

And this is where God comes into the picture. When people get sick, he usually gets blamed. A friend told me a story that illustrates this well: He was standing in the lobby of a ministry where he had been invited to speak. Out of the corner of his eye, he noticed the receptionist was crying, so he asked if he could pray for her. "My dad died recently of a heart attack," she said. "Why did God take him from me?"

"God did not take your dad from you," my friend responded. "God never wanted anyone to die. That is why he told Adam and Eve not to eat from the tree of the knowledge of good and evil. And he still does not like it when anyone dies, because it was never his will." As they were speaking, the Holy Spirit put a picture in his mind of a man smoking a cigarette, so he asked the young woman, "Was your dad a chain smoker?"

"Yes," she said.

"And did he have heart disease?"

"Yes."

"And was his heart attack related to his heart disease?"

"Yes."

"So, you see," my friend said, "God did not want your dad to die. Your dad died because of his bad health habits."[1]

Some ignorant decisions affect vast numbers of people, even whole nations. During the early 1900s, a decision was made to introduce cane toads to curb the growth of the grey-backed

"Frenchi" beetles that were destroying sugarcane crops in Queensland, Australia. With the best of intentions, 102 cane toads were imported from Hawaii in June 1935 and released in the cane fields. It soon became clear the experiment had failed. The cane toads did eat insects, but the real problem was the beetle larvae, which consume the roots. Who knew? The importation of cane toads introduced an entirely new problem because cane toads have no natural predators in Australia. At last count, it's estimated cane toads now outnumber the human population by almost ten to one. And by the way, we still have a beetle problem.

Even mature and well-meaning men and women sometimes make unwise decisions that negatively impact the lives of others. Moses was one of them. He genuinely cared for his people and would have never done anything to deliberately harm them, but his micromanaging leadership style did exactly that. He wanted the people to live according to God's laws, but he assumed he was the only one qualified to counsel them. This forced those needing help to wait in long lines, sometimes all day in the hot sun, until Moses was able to meet with them personally (Ex. 18:13).

Moses was starting to burn out too, that is, until his father-in-law arrived for a visit. Jethro was a seasoned old man with a lot of experience. He immediately saw what the problem was. "What are you really accomplishing here?" he asked Moses. "Why are you trying to do all this alone while everyone stands around you from morning till evening?" (Ex. 18:14 NLT) He then gave him a detailed plan to take care of the issue. Thank God for people with common sense!

Other examples abound. Some are cultural in nature, and others religious. Most of the "religious" ones come from a warped concept of the character of God. When people see him as distant and unloving, they go to unreasonable extremes to placate him.

The annual Vegetarian Festival in Phuket, Thailand, for example, requires participants to pierce their cheeks with spears, knives, and swords, then walk on hot coals and climb ladders laden with sharp objects. It is a horrible ritual, but people do it year after year because they believe the piercings protect them from evil and bring good luck to their families.

In the Indian State of Maharashtra, a baby-dropping ritual is performed at the temple. Toddlers are dangled from heights of up to fifty feet and then dropped into a sheet held by men below. Some children are permanently handicapped and others die, but the practice continues to this day because it is thought to bring good health and prosperity to the family of the baby.

The Amazonian tribe of Satere-Mawe do not consider boys to be men until they venture into the jungle with the Medicine man to be stung by bullet ants, and the Ndani tribe of the Baliem Valley in West Papua, New Guinea cut off one of their fingers at funeral ceremonies to demonstrate the depth of their grief for deceased loved ones. And they do it without the use of any anesthetic.

Penance is practiced around the globe in nominally Christian nations too during Lent and Holy Week. Self-flagellation and various forms of self-inflicted pain is thought to achieve God's forgiveness. When I lived in Argentina, I witnessed people crawling on their hands and knees for thirty-plus miles between Buenos Aires and Our Lady of Luján Cathedral. Bleeding and in obvious pain, they would soldier on, believing their sacrificial act would absolve the guilt they felt for their sins. If only they had understood that the God of the Bible looks for a broken spirit, not a broken body (Ps. 51:16-17).

And finally, there are those who feel guilt and condemnation over decisions that were made long ago. They keep second-guessing themselves, wondering if the outcome could have been different. "If only I had taken another way home from work," or, "if only I had looked in the other direction first," or, "if only I hadn't let him in." This last one tormented Stephanie Snell for over ten years.

That night of December 8, 2007, she had stayed back after YWAM Denver's Christmas Love Feast while the others went bowling:

"I was still in my dress from the party," she said. "Around 11:30, I heard someone persistently knocking on the front door. I figured it was one of the other YWAMers coming home so I went over and opened it. To my surprise, it was no one I knew. The guy had glasses and was wearing a hat, and his head was down. He said he wanted to come in, but I was hesitant because I didn't recognize him. But then, he told me some names of staff members and said he was visiting for the night. Reluctantly, I let him in. I wish I had never done that.

He asked where the bathroom was … I went upstairs to my bedroom but I felt increasingly uneasy in my spirit. When I mentioned it to some of my roommates, none of them seemed particularly alarmed. I remember feeling really anxious inside, so I decided to go and find Tiffany to tell her what had happened. When I got to the foot of the stairwell, there he was, standing in the hallway looking at pictures on the wall of past schools. My adrenaline shot up and I wanted to turn and run, but I forced myself to smile and carefully turned around to walk away.

"I found Dan, Tiffany's boyfriend, and asked if he knew where she was but he didn't know. Then when I turned around, she was standing there. I explained what had happened and that I had let this guy in who said he had been cleared to stay for the night. I felt like

I had done something wrong, but Tiffany was so sweet about it. She told me she would go and talk to him. I keep racking my brain trying to remember the last thing she said. It was something like 'Don't worry sweetheart' or 'I'll take care of it sweetie.' I wish I could remember. All I know is that she spoke in her usual loving way and made me feel at ease. I still felt that something was wrong so I asked Dan to go with her. That was the last time I saw either of them that night—and the last time I ever saw Tiff.

"I can't remember the exact time we heard the gun-shots. One of the students came running in and said there was blood all over the hallway upstairs. I remember being grabbed by one of the other students and we barricaded ourselves in the utility storage closet. We waited and prayed, but all I could do was cry quietly.

"It seemed that we were in there for ages when a SWAT team stormed through and found us. After asking some questions, they moved us to the garage and told us to sit on the floor. We sat on the cold cement for the longest time. Everyone was talking about what had happened and then someone asked, 'Who was it that let him in?' Finally, they put us all on buses and transported us down to the police station for questioning. When it was my turn, they asked me exactly what happened and what Matthew looked like—and that's when I realized he hadn't been caught.

"They wanted me to sit with a sketch artist and I was trying so hard to get everything right. I was the one who let him in and had had the most interaction with him. I kept thinking, *I have to get this right.* In the early hours of the morning, around daybreak, they let us go and we headed up to our campus in the mountains. Everyone was talking about how horrible it was that something like this could happen at YWAM, and it didn't take long for the question to come up again, 'Who let him in?' Everyone wanted to know the whole story, but I wasn't ready to say anything. I felt so guilty."[2]

PERSONAL APPLICATION

Have you apologized to those who have been negatively impacted by your negligence?

Acknowledging our wrongdoing is not only the right thing to do, it is one of the keys to moving forward, both in our own lives and the lives of those who have been negatively impacted by our words or actions. If what took place was your fault, the least you can do is say sorry. I recommend you apologize in person rather than through an email or a letter. Unfortunately, we live in a day when people take legal action against others for little or no reason, so it's best not to leave a permanent record of what took place. Despite this fact, the act of apologizing should never be overlooked.

What are you doing to put the incident behind you?

The second important step is to stop replaying the event over and over again in your mind. There is usually nothing we can do to change an outcome after the fact, so finding a healthy way to move forward is crucial. "Forgetting what lies behind," is what the New Testament encourages us to do (Phil. 3:13), but sometimes we need others to lend a helping hand. If you are struggling with depression or suicidal thoughts, you might need to see a professional counselor. The sooner you get help the sooner you will be able to get on with the rest of your life.

Are you paying attention to the Holy Spirit's prompting?

And finally, from now on train your ear to be attentive to the gentle whisper of the Holy Spirit. "Pray without ceasing" is not just a quaint cliché (1 Thess. 5:17). Paul's implication here is that we stay connected with God every moment of the day. Prayer is the biblical term for communication with him, and it's especially important when we don't know what to do. None of us can anticipate the outcome of *all* our actions, nor the actions of others, but God can, and he will speak to us if we take the time to listen.

Praying without ceasing is basically the inclusion of God in *every* area of our lives. It is the passionate pursuit of his presence before, during, and after every decision we make. If we would only block out the other voices—the voice of our own desires, the voice of others' opinions, and the voice of our adversary the devil, who is always trying to lead us astray, the only voice that would remain is that still, small voice of God's Spirit, whispering his directives at each turn in the road: "This is the way, walk in it" (Isa. 30:21). Think of all the bad things that could be avoided if we all chose to live this way.

My friend, Paul Dangtoumda, was attentive to that gentle whisper, and it saved his life. He was traveling by bus to the north of the nation of Nigeria. He and a friend were sitting in the last row of the vehicle when the driver pulled over to help another bus that had a flat tire. "Within a few minutes of the bus stopping, the Lord spoke to me," Paul said. "Get off the bus now!" Paul told his friend what he was sensing, so they made their way to the front and quickly got off. "As soon as we stepped off the bus, I saw a vehicle pulling up behind us with its lights dimmed," Paul said. "Then, several men got out and I could see they had automatic weapons. At that, we both dove into the bushes at the side of the road and began crawling away as fast as we could. It was painful, as thorns and sharp branches dug into our arms and legs but at that point we didn't care. Within a few seconds the gunfire began and we could hear people screaming. I lost sight of my friend, but continued crawling through the dense undergrowth until I finally came to a clearing. My friend had made it out too, and although we were both bleeding and in shock, we were okay. We later found out most of the people had been killed, and their belongings stolen. Thank God for his protection," Paul said. "There is no question we would have both been shot if we had not listened to the prompting of the Holy Spirit."[3]

CHAPTER SIX

Disregard for the laws of nature

*If you fear nothing, you are not brave. You
are merely too foolish to be afraid.*
—LAURELL K. HAMILTON

Our Skiers and Snowboarders Discipleship Training School,
held every winter at our Eagle Rock camp, is no ordinary
school. Students come from all over the world to experience the
radical transformation of a DTS, coupled with the opportunity
to shred some of the best slopes in North America. The school
tuition includes season passes to three world-class ski resorts,
and on Sundays, we get to share our faith in an outdoor service
on one of them we call *Church on the Hill.* It's the experience of
a lifetime for any on-fire-for-God skier or snowboarder. But all
that action is still not enough for some of the staff and students
who build makeshift ramps at the camp to work on their jumps
and tricks.

Two of our Canadian guys, Josh and Mitch, had built one
such ramp to jump over the gravel road leading up to our property. Josh had done jumps like this hundreds of times before,

and on this day the snow conditions were perfect. But on his first attempt, everything went wrong. Mitch was riding behind him filming the entire jump. "It seemed like the ramp we built gave out a bit just as he took off," Mitch told me later. As soon as he was airborne, Josh realized he was in trouble. He almost made it to the other side, but he landed flat on his back on the edge of the road and everything went numb. He couldn't move his arms or legs, or feel his fingers, as he lay face down in the snow.

Mitch rushed to the aid of his friend. He knew enough to not move him, so he gently brushed the snow away from his mouth so he could breathe. That action probably saved his life, one of the paramedics remarked later. Within the hour, a chopper had landed in the clearing above the road to whisk Josh away to a Denver-area hospital. He has never walked again.

A FIXED ENVIRONMENT

When God created the physical world, he created it with a fixed environment. In other words, he put physical laws in place that would function in a precise and consistent manner, making them predictable. This is called "causality" in physics, or the law of "cause and effect." This law states that every cause *must* have a resulting effect. The law of gravity functions this way. Throw an object up in the air and it will come down to the earth again. You can count on it. The object cannot independently decide to stay afloat, because it is subject to the gravitational force of the earth. If God had not created the environment with fixed laws like this, it would be unpredictable, and lead to a tremendous amount of insecurity in all of us.

The great test pilot Chuck Yeager was a lot like Josh. He was always "pushing the edge of the envelope" as he described it. On December 10, 1963, he was attempting to fly his Lockheed NF-104 supersonic jet to over 100,000 feet when the "envelope" snapped back. The jet stalled and went into a tail-spin. The terrifying spin and crash that nearly took Yeager's life are detailed in Tom Wolfe's epic *The Right Stuff.* Sadly, many risk takers are not as fortunate as Chuck when they have attempted to push the edge of the envelope, and more often than not, God is blamed for the outcome. But what people tend to overlook is that God does not manage the environment on a day-to-day basis. Instead, he put physical laws in place that we humans must learn to respect.

After God created the physical world, he created man and gave him free rein over the planet. He told him to use his creativity and intelligence to master the physical world. "Fill the earth and subdue it," he told him (Gen. 1:28). And, over time, that is what happened. Man discovered how to use fire to cook food and warm his house in winter. He invented the wheel to move heavy objects from one place to another. He harnessed the power of electricity to generate energy and light. He built bridges and skyscrapers, and telescopes. He found cures for different kinds of diseases and began to surgically replace damaged organs. He built planes that could fly thousands of miles at supersonic speeds and began to explore the vastness of space. All of this is exactly what God had envisioned for man, made possible, by the predictability of the environment around him. The entire physical world functions on this premise.

The gravitational force of the moon, for example, pulls oceans upwards, creating a bulge in the water that results in high tides in the parts of the earth that face the moon, and low tides in the areas that don't. Every surfer is thankful for this amazing phenomenon. Wind functions under the laws of cause and effect too. On the surface, wind seems to be random, but it is not. The earth's surface is made up of different types of land and water that absorb the heat of the sun at different rates, and the result is that it moves the air around us. We call it wind.

Meteorologist Edward Lorenz went so far as to suggest that even the smallest changes in one state of what he called, "a deterministic nonlinear system," could result in large differences in a latter state. He called it *The Butterfly Effect*. Could a butterfly flapping its wings in Brazil trigger a hurricane in Texas, he asked? Probably not—a causation that small resulting in an effect that large is probably not possible, but what *is* certain is that every effect comes from an originating cause. God created the whole universe to operate on this premise so we could depend upon it as we went about our daily lives.

A PROBABLE OUTCOME

Although the physical world is predictable, man is unpredictable. God gave *us* the ability to use, but conversely, the ability to abuse, the laws of nature, which makes suffering a possible outcome. The fire that warms your home in winter could burn it down if you are not careful with how you manage the fire. The energy generated from splitting an atom can supply electricity to an entire city, but if used irresponsibly, it can demolish that same city in a matter of seconds. The automobile that moves people safely from one place to another could cause them great bodily harm if the driver exceeds the speed limit and crashes into a tree. It is not God causing these things to happen. It is the result of carelessness related to the fixed environment.

Clearly God has the power to protect us from any and every bad thing that could happen to us, but instead of stepping in each time we do something foolish, he gave us the ability to make intelligent decisions on our own. He wanted us to rule the earth. Could he step in? Yes. Could he micromanage every detail? Of course, but that is not the way he designed the universe.

Philosopher John Hick hypothesized what a world devoid of physical injury and pain might look like: "The consequences would be very far-reaching," he said. "Nature would have to work 'special providences' instead of running according to general laws, which men must learn to respect on penalty of pain and death. The laws of nature would have to be extremely flexible. Sometimes an object would be hard and solid, sometimes soft. One can at least begin to imagine such a world. It is evident that our ethical concepts would have no meaning in it."[1]

If, for example, the notion of harming someone is an essential element in the concept of wrong action, in this hedonistic paradise there could be no wrong actions—nor any right actions in distinction from wrong. Courage and fortitude would have no point in an environment in which there is, by definition, no danger or difficulty. Generosity, kindness, the *agape* aspect of love, prudence, unselfishness, and all other ethical notions, which presuppose life in a stable environment, could not even be formed. "Consequently," Hick concludes, "such a world, however well it might promote pleasure, would be very ill adapted for the development of the moral qualities of human personality. In relation to this purpose it would be the worst of all possible worlds."[2]

"If matter has a fixed nature and obeys constant laws," C. S. Lewis argued, "not all states of matter will be equally agreeable to the wishes of a given soul. If fire comforts the body at a certain distance, it will destroy it when that distance is reduced."[3] The environment cannot change to fit the preferences of every individual. What is agreeable to one person might not be as agreeable to the next. Most husbands and wives face this problem in their own homes. It is certainly the case in mine. When the house is warm enough for me, it is usually too cold for my wife, but when it is warm enough for her, it is too warm for me. The air does not change its temperature to accommodate the wishes of every individual person it touches.

Along these lines Yancey uses the example of wood:

"This wonderful material God gave to us forms the main substance of trees, which bears fruit, supports leaves to provide shade, and shelters birds and squirrels. Even when taken from the tree, wood is valuable. We use it as fuel to warm ourselves, and as construction material to build houses and furniture. The essential properties of wood—make possible these useful functions. But as soon as you plant a tree with those properties in a world peopled by free human beings, you introduce the possibility of abuse. A free man may pick up a chunk of wood and take advantage of its firmness by bashing the head of another man. God could reach down each time and transform the properties of wood into those of sponge, so that the club would bounce off lightly. But that is not what he is about in the world. He has set into motion fixed laws that can be perverted to evil by our misguided freedom."[4]

SOME THINGS HAPPEN BY CHANCE

Some suffering related to the laws of nature is entirely circumstantial. Unintentionally, people find themselves in the wrong place at the wrong time—like the woman from Manitoba, visiting her brother on the 105th floor of the Twin Towers the morning of September 11th, 2001, or the tourists sunbathing on the beaches of Phuket, Thailand the day after Christmas, 2004, or John and Catherine Bourke, a young Irish couple who bought one-way tickets on the maiden voyage of the Titanic in 1912. What did any of them do to deserve the tragic outcome of their choices? Nothing. They were just in the wrong place at the wrong time.

This perspective reflects the view of several biblical passages. For example, Jesus used the term "by chance" in his parable of the Good Samaritan. "*By chance* a priest was going down the road," he said (Luke 10:31). The word he used is *sugkuria,* which means *coincidentally*. In another passage, we find a similar word, which also means "by chance." Acts 17:17 tells us Paul was witnessing in the public square to those "who *happened* to be there." Because some things happen by chance, some suffer and die through no fault of their own.

Jesus rejected the idea that all suffering comes from God, a prevalent belief in Middle Eastern culture dating all the way back to the days of Job. When they told him Pilate had killed a group of Galilean pilgrims visiting Jerusalem, he asked, "Do you think that they were worse sinners than all of the others? Is that why they suffered?" It was a rhetorical question, of course, but just to make sure they understood what he was saying he added: "Not at all!" Then, he referenced another incident where eighteen people died when a tower collapsed on top of them. "Do you think that they were worse offenders than all the others who lived in Jerusalem?" he asked. "No," (Luke 13:4-5). Jesus made it absolutely clear that those who perished had done nothing wrong. He doesn't say so, but perhaps the tower fell simply because it was constructed poorly and succumbed to the gravitational force of the earth at the exact moment the eighteen pilgrims were standing beneath it. Some things happen by chance. It is the reality of living in a world with a fixed environment.

In his book, *Creative Suffering*, Swiss physician Paul Tournier says he used to judge successes or tragedies as either good or evil, but he has since changed his perspective. He now believes circumstances, whether fortunate or unfortunate, are morally neutral. "They simply are what they are," he says. "What matters most is how we respond to them. Good and evil in the moral sense, do not reside in things but always in persons."

GOD IS THE EASIEST TARGET

I am reminded of a friend who was driving his pickup truck on the freeway one afternoon when he realized he was about to miss his intended exit. Instead of driving to the next off-ramp several miles down the road, which would have been the smart thing to do, he tried to save five minutes by veering across three lanes of traffic. He didn't make it. He rolled his vehicle three or four times, coming to a complete stop just a few feet past the off-ramp. Thankfully, he was not injured, but his first response was to pray, "Lord, what are you trying to teach me?"

"Don't blame me for that," the Lord responded, "I wasn't the one who tried to take that exit when it was too late."

Satan was fully aware of God's ability to control the forces of nature when he dared Jesus to jump from the temple roof to prove he was the Son of God. "God will command his angels to protect you," he reasoned with him (Matt. 4:6). Was Satan telling the truth? Yes, God could do that, but he does not usually intervene when we abuse the laws he put in place. He expects us, instead, to make wise and intelligent decisions, and when we don't, suffering is often the outcome.

Although some people blame God for the tragic events in their lives, Josh Bergen, the snowboarder injured at our Eagle Rock camp, is not one of them:

> "2016 was one of the hardest years of my life," he told me a year or so after the accident. "Day after day, I kept feeling sorry for myself as I hid away in my apartment in Winnipeg. I really struggled with God's love during that time. Then God spoke to me from the passage where he told Paul his grace was sufficient for him, and that his power is made perfect in weakness. I feel now that I'm partaking with Christ in *his* suffering and that makes it all the more worth it. If it was worth it for him to suffer for me then he is worthy of any suffering I could encounter." Wow, what faith![5]

FAITH IS NOT JUST FOR GOOD THINGS

The point we must not fail to grasp is that faith is sometimes most evident in people like Josh. The great heroes of the faith mentioned in the book of Hebrews, are acknowledged for their mighty exploits, like conquering kingdoms, stopping the mouths of lions, and putting entire enemy armies to flight. Some of them escaped the edge of the sword, and others raised their loved ones from the dead—all by faith. But then it goes on to mention those who were persecuted, imprisoned, and martyred. What could this mean? Some escaped the edge of the sword while others were killed by it (Heb. 11:34-37). What was the difference between them? Both groups had faith (Heb. 11:39). And the only way to make sense of this passage is for us to conclude that faith is not just for the good things. It is also evident in people like Josh, who face the challenges of life head-on without blaming God for their horrible circumstances.

PERSONAL APPLICATION

*It is better to be careful 100 times than to
get killed once*—Mark Twain

***Are you engaging in activities that are putting
your life or the lives of others at risk?***

You and I have only one life to live, so it is important we make it last the distance. This is especially important for those with risk-taking personalities. "Most of the time, individuals who engage in risky behavior don't even think that what they are doing is risky," explains Angela Bryan, assistant professor of psychology at the University of Colorado. "None of us think we will have an accident or get a disease, but risk-takers often do not even consider it at all." On personality tests, risk-takers tended to score high on impulsivity and low on things like conscientiousness and self-control. "Teenagers are the most at risk because they feel the need to explore their limits and abilities. It's part of their pathway to becoming independent adults," says Terrie Moffitt, of the University of Wisconsin. "But this testing of boundaries puts them at a higher risk."

The Bible warns us not to test God. This is what Jesus said when Satan dared him to jump from the roof of the temple (Matt. 4:7). "Ekpeirazó," is the word he used, which means, "to tempt the Lord," or "to put God's *power* to the test." It is not that God is looking to punish us for our foolish behavior. On the contrary, he wants what is best for us. Putting his power to the test is when we do something so foolish it would require his direct intervention to save us. Instead he wants us to use good judgment. In Ephesians the point is clear: "Be careful how you live. Don't live like fools, but like those who are wise" (Eph. 5:15 NLT).

Are you willing to trust God in every situation?

Faith is evident in times of difficulty, not just in times of blessing and provision. It is put on full display when we hold on to God, rather than distancing ourselves from him when things go wrong. "His work is perfect, for all his ways are justice," Moses declared when he was informed he would not be going into the Promised Land after all (Deut. 32:4). This had been his dream for years, and God had just informed him it wasn't going to happen (Deut. 32:1). Yet he trusted God despite the circumstances. Trusting God at all times is not a blind leap of faith. It is faith anchored in the knowledge of who God is.

In his book, "How Should We Then Live?" Dr. Francis Schaeffer describes a scenario in which a group of tourists are climbing on a bare rock high in the Swiss Alps. Suddenly and unexpectedly the fog rolls in. The guide turns to the group and says that ice is forming on the ledge and he sees no way for them to safely descend from the mountain. "Before morning we will probably freeze to death up here," he says. Simply to keep warm the guide keeps them moving in the dense fog further out on the shoulder until none of them have any idea where they are.

After an hour or so, one of the tourists asks to the guide, "Suppose I dropped off the cliff and hit a ledge ten feet down in the fog? What would happen to me?" The guide thinks for a moment, and then says there is a good chance he might make it until morning and thus live. So, with absolutely no certainty in the outcome, the man drops off the ledge. "This, Schaeffer says, "is a blind leap of faith." But that is not what God asks of us.

Suppose, instead, after the group had ventured onto the ledge, they heard a voice calling out in the distance: "You cannot see me, but I know exactly where you are from your voices. I am on another ridge. I have lived in these mountains for over sixty years and know every foot of them. I assure you that ten feet below you there is a ledge, and if you hang off and drop onto it, you can make it through the night and I will come and get you in the morning."

If the group decides to trust the man, it is still scary, but it is no longer a blind leap of faith. It is faith in the man's word and in his character. And this is the faith God asks of us when things go wrong in our lives—a faith based in who he is and what he has promised.

CHAPTER SEVEN

The Kingdom of Darkness

There is no neutral ground in the universe;
every square inch, every split second, is
claimed by God and counterclaimed by
Satan.

—C. S. LEWIS

Although invisible to the naked eye, there is a spiritual battle, taking place in the heavenly realm above us. In its broadest sense it is a battle for control of cities and nations, and for the right to rule this world, but it is also a battle for marriages and families, and for the individual souls of men, women, and children. It is not, however, a physical battle, and cannot be won by physical means, which has led some to question if the idea of a spiritual battle is just a figment of some people's imagination. But make no mistake. The battle is not only real, but it is raging all around us as we speak. The scriptures tell us, "We are not fighting against flesh-and-blood enemies, but against evil rulers and authorities of the unseen world" (Eph. 6:12 NLT).

The adversaries in this invisible conflict are powerful, supernatural beings described with ominous names like, "thrones, dominions, rulers, and authorities" (Col. 1:16). And then there are demons, which are possibly a different type of spiritual being altogether. Jesus spent a lot of time casting them out of people when he was on earth (Mark 1:34).

SATAN

Their commander in chief is Satan, who is a fallen angel. Prior to his fall his name was Lucifer, which means, "shining one" in Latin (Isa. 14:12). He was one of God's highest-ranking officials along with at least two other archangels, Michael and Gabriel. Together, these leader-angels served God as worshipers (Rev. 4:8), messengers (Dan. 9:22; Luke 1:11) and mighty warriors (Rev. 12:7-9). They were powerful and magnificent in their appearance (Ezek. 28: 12-14), but then one of them fell. Every moral being must make this decision at one point or another— to give allegiance to God or to self. Lucifer chose himself.[1]

While the book of Revelation tells of many events that will take place in the future, some seem to be *flashbacks* of events that happened in the past. One such event is a battle between Satan and the archangel Michael. Satan wanted to be equal with God (Isa. 14:14). He was delusional, of course, but pride is a great deceiver, and those who indulge in it will eventually believe the lie they are greater than they really are. The next thing we read, Satan has been defeated, and he, and his hoard of fallen angels have been thrown out of heaven and sent to the earth (Rev. 12:9). And this is where they have remained until this day.

WHAT HE IS REALLY LIKE

The Bible depicts Satan as the leader of an army of spiritual powers. He is called the *ruler* of demons (Matt. 9:34), and fallen angels are referred to as *his* angels (Matt. 25:41). Jesus described him as "the prince of this world" *(archōn)*, which in Greco-Roman times was a title ascribed to the highest-ranking official in a city or region. God is clearly the *ultimate* ruler over his creation, but Satan is named as the *functional* ruler over several places on earth. Even more stunning is John's claim that *the whole world* has come under his control (1 John. 5:19).

He has many names because of his many disguises, but when we put them all together, a picture begins to emerge of what he is really like. He is "the god of this world" (2 Cor. 4:4), "the prince of the power of the air" (Eph. 2:2), and the "father of lies" (John 8:44). In the book of Revelation, he showed up as a dragon with seven heads and ten horns (Rev. 12:3), and in the Garden of Eden, he came disguised as a serpent (Gen. 3:1).

The most frightening of all descriptions, however, says that he, "disguises himself as an angel of light" (2 Cor. 11:14). In other words, he comes across as someone who is trustworthy and holy, when in reality, Jesus said, "he was a murderer from the beginning" (John 8:44).

Satan has an impressive résumé of obstruction and harassment of God's people, but let's not attribute more power to him than he really has. He is not infinite like God. He is a finite created being, the opposite, C. S. Lewis pointed out, not of God, but of Michael the archangel. George Lucas was correct that there is a dark side out there, but what he didn't get right is that it is not the mirror image of God. That is what he wants us to believe, but it is all a façade. At the end of time we will look upon him and ask in amazement: "Can this be the one who shook the earth and made the kingdoms of the world tremble?" (Isa.14:16 NLT).

Satan knows many things, but he doesn't know everything. The Bible makes it clear God is the only one who knows the thoughts and desires of men's hearts (1 Kings 8:39). How, then, has he become such an expert at knowing how to attack us? The answer to this question is not that complicated. All he has to do is observe the things we do and say, but in terms of his ability to read our minds, no, he does not have that ability. Also, his presence is limited to space and time much like we are, but he can obviously get around much faster than we can because he can fly. The Bible describes him as a cherub (Ezek. 28:14), which is a type of supernatural being, possessing both human and animal characteristics (Ezek. 1:10). These beings have multiple sets of eyes (Ezek. 1:18), and several wings (Rev. 4:8), which enable them to fly at high speeds from one place to another. But he is not omnipresent, which forces him to delegate many assignments to lower ranking demons and fallen angels under his control. He also infiltrates human authority structures, like governments, educational systems, and the media, which become tools for evil in his hand.

Satan has always sought to use human beings to carry out his evil schemes (2 Tim. 2:26). We are told *he* was the one who possessed Judas Iscariot in the days leading up to Jesus' betrayal and apprehension (Luke 22:3). Clearly he wasn't willing to risk delegating such an important task to a low-ranking demon, so he took matters into his own hands. We see his fingerprints all over the events leading up to Jesus' arrest and crucifixion. In his demonically inspired song, "Sympathy for the Devil," Mick Jagger eerily describes Satan's blatant boast:

> *I've been around for a long, long year*
> *Stole many a man's soul to waste*
> *And I was 'round when Jesus Christ*
> *Had his moment of doubt and pain*
> *Made damn sure that Pilate*
> *Washed his hands and sealed his fate.*[2]

But what neither Pilate, nor Satan, nor Mick Jagger for that matter, understood was that Jesus' death was all part of God's master plan to take back the power of death from the devil (Heb. 2:14).

Satan is constantly looking for ways to get back at God by lashing out at those he loves. This includes every person on earth, of course, because God loves the *whole* world (John 3:16). He is portrayed as a cunning deceiver who leads people astray, and as, "the accuser of our brothers" (Rev. 12:10). In a global sense, every generation must face him in the form of the spirit of the antichrist and world domination. "This was the spirit behind those who had ambition to rule the world such as Napoleon or Hitler," argues John Dawson. "They usurped the place that belongs only to God: 'The earth is the Lord's and all its fullness' (Ps. 24:1). "A praying church should face this spirit and drive it off long before we find ourselves in another world at war."[3]

WHEN WILL HE FINALLY BE BROUGHT TO JUSTICE?

The question some ask is if Jesus defeated Satan on the cross, why is he still freely roaming the earth and carrying out his evil schemes? If he was truly defeated, the argument goes, shouldn't he be rendered powerless by now? Despite the difficulties this matter presents, C. Peter Wagner makes an important observation that bears mentioning. In his book, *Warfare Prayer*, he compares our current reality with Abraham Lincoln's Emancipation Proclamation.

"From 1863 on, black Americans have been granted full citizenship and social equality with all other Americans. No one in America questions the legality of the Emancipation Proclamation ... Virtually all Americans, however, recognize and are embarrassed that today African

Americans as a social unit do not actually enjoy full social equality alongside other Americans. It has taken time to implement in practice what was done legally … It took almost 100 years for some states to get rid of Jim Crow laws, which prevented blacks from voting, kept them out of certain restaurants, and sat them at the back of buses."

"In a similar way," Wagner argues, "Jesus' death on the cross was the Emancipation Proclamation for the entire human race. However, 2,000 years later, multitudes are not yet saved and huge segments of the world's peoples continue to live in social disaster areas. Just as I want to see victims of social injustice in our nation receive their rightful freedom, so I also want to see victims of satanic oppression around the world freed from Satan's evil grasp. In order to do either, however, it's not enough to look back to legitimate legal transactions made hundreds or thousands of years ago."[4]

One day, Satan will be required to stand before God and answer for all the evil things he has done on earth. Like a convicted criminal, he will once-and-for-all be sentenced to an eternal prison called *the lake of fire* (Rev. 20:10). In the meantime, however, God has decided that we, the Church, should take the lead in this spiritual battle. Seriously? Was this the best strategy God could come up with? Why not use Michael, Gabriel, or some of the other angelic warriors to lead the fight? They are much more powerful than we are and better equipped to take on the devil. Well, they are helping too, but evidently God wants for us to be at the forefront. He tells *us* to go into the whole world and preach the Gospel (Mark 16:15). He tells *us* to pray (Matt. 9:38). He instructed *us* to bind the strongman and set his captives free (Matt. 12:29).

SPIRITUAL FORCES OF EVIL

The next echelon of power in the kingdom of darkness is what is called, "spiritual forces of evil in the heavenly places" (Eph. 6:12). Who exactly are these spiritual forces, and what are they attempting to do? To answer this question, we need to go back to the beginning.

The Bible tells us God created everything (Gen. 1:1). Some of his creation dwells on earth, while other parts of it live in the heavenly realm. Some of it is visible, and some invisible (Col. 1:16). In many ways the two realms are interconnected. Much more than a lot of people think. The dominant materialistic world does not know what to do with this concept. Those of us who have grown up in a predominantly western context find it difficult to conceptualize there could be another realm subsisting simultaneously alongside our visible one, but that is how the Bible describes it (1 Cor. 15:40).

There must be dozens of different types of these spiritual beings around us, all with distinct roles and job descriptions. The ones Ezekiel saw had four wings (Ezek. 1:5-6), whereas the ones in John's vision had six (Rev. 4:6-8). We know there are at least a hundred million of them because their number is said to be, "ten thousand times ten thousand" (Rev. 5:11 NIV). It's not entirely clear why God created so many, but what *is* clear is they were not evil to begin with. They were made *by* God and *for* God (Col. 1:16), but like us, they were created with free wills.

Somewhere along the way, a third of them rebelled against God (Rev. 12:4; Jude 1:6). Some took over cities and nations (Dan. 10:20), and others entered into an unnatural sexual union with women, giving birth to a whole new race of mutant creatures called *The Nephilim* (Gen. 6:1-4). The New Testament clumps them all together in what is called, "the domain of darkness" (Col. 1:13), and in another place, "the dominion of Satan" (Acts 26:18). "Together," Thomas Yoder Neufeld concludes, "They provide a seamless web of reality hostile to God."[5]

EXPECT A CONFRONTATION

If you don't meet the devil on your journey, it is because you are going the same direction—African proverb

Forces of evil seek to control the spiritual landscape, be it a nation like Persia or Greece (Dan. 10:20), or a significant urban center like Ephesus (1 Cor. 15:32). For us today, this would be like saying the nation of Venezuela or the city of Paris had come under the influence of an evil presence. Once they gain the upper hand in the spiritual realm, the physical realm follows closely behind, usually in the form of people committing evil acts toward other human beings. The evil seems to come out of nowhere, but usually, it has been there for a while, steadily gaining ground until it manifests in a tangible way. This is what the world found out when the Nazis took control of Germany. Up until that point, no one could have predicted the horrors that were in store. Even Winston Churchill said that if Hitler had died before 1938, he would have been remembered as one of the greatest leaders in history because of all the wonderful things he did to help rebuild that nation. But as soon as he gave himself over to the spirit of world domination, everything changed.

In the words of Carl Jung: "One man, who is obviously 'possessed,' has infected a whole nation ... a god has taken possession of the Germans."[6] And Walter Wink concurs, writing that, "Hitler and his Nazi regime incarnated the demonic in such an intense way that almost anybody who did not fall under its spell could see, and had to admit, the reality of a transcendent force of evil in their activity."[7]

The apostle Paul encountered similar forces of evil when he tried to enter the city of Ephesus, describing them as *"wild beasts"* hell-bent on stopping him (1 Cor. 15:32). Ephesus was one of the primary centers for commerce in the ancient world with a population of a quarter of a million during the Roman time. That was a megacity back then, especially when we consider the entire population of the world numbered less than the current population of the United States. Ephesus was a key urban center that would eventually become the home of one of the largest and most dynamic churches in the New Testament era. Is it any wonder why Paul encountered opposition when he tried to go there? Whenever we pose a threat to Satan's kingdom, we should expect a confrontation. Spiritual warfare is usually an indicator, not that we're on the wrong track, but that we're on the right one.

A SPIRIT OF FEAR IN WEST AFRICA

Several years ago, I was on my way to minister in West Africa. The final leg of my journey was on a small regional air carrier from Conakry, Guinea to Freetown, Sierra Leone. When I landed in Conakry, I was told I would not be able to complete my journey because the airline was no longer in existence. I had a paper ticket from my travel agent back in Denver, but it was worthless. Fortunately, there was a biweekly ferry leaving the next morning, so I caught a cab to the port area and checked into a hotel for the night. That evening was a nightmare.

I couldn't sleep for more than 15 to 20 minutes at a time because of an overwhelming sense that something bad was about to happen. I am not usually a fearful person, but on this occasion I was terrified. Finally, after what seemed like an eternity, I could see it was starting to get light outside. I ran down to the front desk, paid my bill, and hurried off to catch the ferry to Freetown. I couldn't wait to get out of there. It took me several days to fully comprehend what had happened. It was not a fear from within that was troubling me. It was a spirit of fear in the city and I had entered into its territorial domain. Five years later, I recognized the same spirit when the shootings took place.

The physical and spiritual worlds are a lot more interconnected than many of us realize. We read of gang violence, corrupt governments and child abuse, without clearly establishing
the connection to the very real conflict in the unseen realm.[8]
Tribal peoples around the world are not ignorant of these realities. They understand the world is much more than just a physical place. Take for example, the Shuar Indians of eastern
Ecuador. They believe in two levels of reality: the "ordinary"
physical world, which is experienced through our senses, and
the "real" world, which is experienced only occasionally, and
mostly in dreams and shamanic journeys. According to the
Shuar, the genuine cause of events in our "unreal" physical
world is found in the "real" spiritual world, a mostly invisible
dimension of reality that is virtually saturated with spirits.[9]

The Wemale people of Ceram, Indonesia are continually at
war against the *halita*, who are demonic spirits they believe
abduct and eat human beings. They are also constantly waging
war against the spirits of disease they believe inhabit the sky.[10]
Then, there is the Kamwe tribe of northeastern Nigeria who
believe in a Supreme Being called Hyalatamwe, who is perfectly just and created the world "perfect and with no sickness
or death." Evil has risen, they maintain, neither from
Hyalatamwe nor from the good spirits, but from evil spirits
who are almost always associated with certain trees, rivers,
stones and caves.[11]

If we look to history, it's not hard to see similar perspectives
among the Babylonians, Canaanites, Egyptians, Sumerians,
and even the ancient Greek philosophers. Plato, for example,
believed the cosmos was inhabited by good and evil demons,
and these "middle creatures," as he described them, were capable of either benefiting or harming human beings.[12]

I am not suggesting we take our cue from pagan people
groups around the world, but think about it for a moment.

There is no way all of them are making this up. And when you factor in that the Bible also describes this physical-spiritual connection, well, it would be naïve of us to deny its existence altogether. Biblical authors generally assumed the existence of intermediary spiritual or cosmic beings, author Greg Boyd points out. "These beings, variously termed 'gods,' 'angels,' 'principalities and powers,' 'demons,' or, in the earliest strata, 'Leviathan' or some other cosmic monster, can and do wage war against God, wreak havoc on his creation and bring all manner of ills upon humanity."[13]

If we modern Westerners cannot *see* what nearly everyone else outside our little oasis of Western rationalism the last several centuries has seen, then perhaps there is something wrong with our way of seeing. Is it just possible that the intensely materialistic and rationalistic orientation of the Enlightenment has blinded us to certain otherwise obvious realities? Is it just possible that our tendency to assume that the worldview we hold at the present time, as the ultimately true worldview, is actually what is preventing us from seeing significant features of spiritual reality?

THE TERRITORIAL NATURE OF SPIRITUAL FORCES OF EVIL

The gospel of Mark describes a demon-possessed man who would wander through the burial caves howling at night and cutting his body with sharp objects (Mark 5:5). Everything changed the moment Jesus arrived. The man came running down to the shore to meet him. "What is your name?" Jesus asked. "Legion," he replied, "for we are many." Then, the demons begged Jesus not to send them to a different location (Mark 5:10). Why were they concerned about that? What difference would it make if they were sent elsewhere? This, I believe, speaks to the territorial nature of the Kingdom of Darkness.

Territorial spirits provide a canopy under which demons can carry out their evil deeds. When rape, murder, and involvement in the occult are prevalent, it creates a stronghold, which is essentially a place of strength in which demons can thrive. If you enter one of these "places," you will feel it immediately, although you might not recognize it as a spiritual thing at first. It often manifests itself in the form of personal temptation, so it's easy to assume *we* are the ones with the problem. Lust, greed, anger, and loneliness—I have felt all of them at times when I have traveled the world. It is usually most intense when I come into a new location. John Dawson says he, too, is best able to discern the unseen realm when he first arrives in a place because of the stark contrast in atmosphere between the old and the new.[14]

There are numerous scriptural references linking principalities and powers to setbacks in the physical realm, like when the archangel Gabriel told Daniel the spirit prince over the Persian kingdom had withstood him for twenty-one days (Dan. 10:13), or when Paul informed the Thessalonians he had tried to come to them on several occasions but Satan was blocking his way (1 Thess. 2:18). Similarly, if indeed a territorial stronghold had created an environment conducive for demons to thrive in the country of the Gerasenes (Mark 5:1), it would explain why they were resistant to being sent to a different location.

GODS OF THE HILLS AND OF THE PLAINS

Pagan peoples have always understood the close connection between the physical and spiritual realms. Overtones of territorial spirits appear as early as the 15th century B.C. in Canaanite mythology. Each of the ancient gods were said to have had "a dwelling place on a particular sacred mountain, at some inaccessible point where heaven and earth meet. From such mountains, their rule over the land and their influence upon its life were believed to flow."[15]

This scenario was played out in the ancient battle between Ahab, king of Israel, and Ben-Hadad, king of Aram (1 Kings 20: 23-29). The military strategy of the campaign was influenced by the idea of territorial gods. After an initial defeat, the official of the king of Aram advised him, "Their gods are the gods of the hills. That is why they were too strong for us. But if we fight them on the plains, surely we will be stronger than they."[16]

The Arameans understood the territoriality of their gods and initiated military strategies based upon them. The following spring, Aram went to war again, but this time, on the plains of Samaria. Unfortunately for them their army was defeated once again, all because they failed to recognize the God they were fighting, was the God of the whole earth!

UNIDENTIFIED FLYING OBJECTS

The Scriptures reveal a fascinating fact: Angels can transform themselves into the likeness of human beings. Jacob wrestled with what he thought was a man, when in reality, it was an angel (Gen. 32:24), and Joshua too, who was confronted by a warrior with a drawn sword on the eve of the battle for Jericho. He, too, turned out to be an angel (Josh. 5:13). And then there was the time when Abraham showed hospitality to three strangers, not knowing one of them was God, and the other two were angels (Gen. 18:2). There is no question angels have the capacity to take on human form. You and I have almost certainly encountered them at one point or another, "without realizing it," the writer of Hebrews tells us (Heb. 13:2 NLT). We probably assumed we were talking with a human being, when in reality they were not human at all.

Sometimes angels have appeared in their original unaltered state, like the one that announced Jesus' birth to the shepherds (Luke 2:9), or those standing guard at Jesus' tomb (John 20:12). The apostle John saw one of them "flying directly overhead"

(Rev. 14:6), and the living creature Ezekiel saw was unlike anything anyone had ever seen before. It looked like "a wheel within a wheel," he said. And it had "eyes all around" (Ezek. 1:16-18).

The idea that spiritual beings can materialize might be a new concept for some, but it is not a new concept from a biblical standpoint. The question is how would a person living in our day and age describe such an encounter? Consider the testimony of Col. L. Gordon Cooper, one of the seven original astronauts in Project Mercury, which was the first manned space program of the United States: "For a long time I have lived with a secret," he said years after the incident, "a secrecy imposed on all specialists and astronauts. I can now reveal that every day, in the U.S.A., our radar instruments capture objects of form and composition unknown to us. And there are thousands of witness reports and a quantity of documents to prove this, but nobody wants to make them public."[17]

"At one stage we thought it might be necessary to take evasive action to avoid a collision," testified James McDivitt, former United States Air Force pilot and NASA astronaut who flew in the Gemini and Apollo programs. He was commenting on an orbital encounter he and Ed White had with a "weird object" with arm-like extensions, which approached their capsule. Later in the flight, they saw two similar objects over the Caribbean.[18]

For decades the Pentagon was tightlipped about the subject of UFO phenomena, until finally, in December 2018, they acknowledged they have been studying the subject all along through a little-known program called Advanced Aerospace Threat Identification Program. Immediately after they went public the Navy issued new guidelines encouraging their pilots to report such encounters with UFOs.

Physicist J. Lemairtre, summarizes, "We can conclude it is impossible to interpret UFO phenomena in terms of material spaceships as we conceive of them, that is, in terms of manufactured and self-propelled machines." And John Keel, reported to be one of the most respected researchers in this field, noted, "Over and over again, witnesses have told me in hushed tones, 'You know, I don't think the thing I saw was mechanical at all. I got the distinct impression it was *alive.*'"[19]

If angels have this type of transmutational ability, doesn't it make sense the dark angels also have it? There is nothing to suggest their intrinsic nature was altered simply because they went over to Satan's side. This is the most logical explanation for UFO phenomena, not of alien life forms visiting our planet, but of spiritual beings, good and evil, that momentarily materialize and then disappear again into thin air.

DON'T BE INTIMIDATED

I would imagine coming face-to-face with an angelic being would be a terrifying experience, which is probably why they usually start with the words: "Do not be afraid." The good news is most of them are on our side. "Those who are with us are more than those who are with them," the prophet explained to his young apprentice. The young man had seen the enemy marching toward them and was terrified (2 Kings 6:16), but when God opened his eyes, he saw what his master was seeing. The mountain was full of horses and chariots of fire (2 Kings 6:17). Billy Graham says, "If we only had open spiritual eyes, we would see not only a world filled with evil spirits and powers—but also powerful angels with drawn swords, set for our defense."[20]

God is going to win this war. Although he didn't start it, he will finish it. No one knows exactly when, of course, only the Father (Matt. 24:36). In the meantime, he calls on us to bind the strongman and set his prisoners free (Matt. 12:29). It is full-on warfare at the highest level from here on out, and it is happening all around us as we speak. If we are not careful, we could become overwhelmed by the intensity of the battle and lose sight of what is really important: God promises to be with us every step of the way: "I will never leave you nor forsake you," he said (Heb. 13:5). That fact alone is a good enough reason not to be intimidated when we come face-to-face with the powers of darkness (Heb. 13:6).

TAKING THE LEAD

I want to live my life in such a way that when I get out of bed in the morning, the devil says, "Aw sh*t, he's up!"—Steve Maraboli

Jesus sends us out in his name. He said, "all authority in heaven and on earth has been given to me, therefore, go and make disciples ..." (Matt. 28:18-19). Many sermons have been preached on the second part of Jesus' commission, "go and make disciples," but let's not miss its strategic connection to the first part. Clearly, what makes our "going" successful is that we are doing so in Jesus' authority rather than our own.

He calls the Church to take the lead in this battle. We are to be on the offensive. George Ladd points out that in the conflict motif between Satan and the kingdom of God, God is the aggressor, and Satan is on the defensive."[21] It's not the other way around. This is why Jesus could say to Simon Peter that the *"gates of Hades"* would not prevail against the Church (Matt. 16:18). *"Hades"* was the standard term for the underworld, the realm of darkness and death in Hellenistic culture, and city gates were the places where government officials met and important military decisions were made. By using the term *"gates of Hades,"* Jesus was metaphorically referring to the command center of the kingdom of darkness.

Considering this: The battle lines have already been drawn. Satan and his hoard of fallen angels on one side, and the Church, aided by God's heavenly host, on the other—both contending for the same piece of real estate: planet earth.

ANGELIC ASSIGNMENTS

God has not left us alone on this earth. He is with us every step of the way through the indwelling of his Holy Spirit, but also, through the presence of powerful angelic forces.

Some are ministering spirits sent to serve us (Heb. 1:14), while others have been tasked to watch over us (Ps. 91:11). The Reverend John G. Patton witnessed this first-hand when he and his wife were missionaries in the New Hebrides Islands of the South Pacific. One night, hostile natives surrounded their missionary headquarters, intent on burning it to the ground and killing them. John and his wife prayed all night for God's protection. And he did. When daylight arrived, they looked out the window and saw their attackers had left.

A year later the chief of the tribe came to Christ. Remembering what had happened, Pastor Patton asked what had kept him and his men from burning down their house and killing them. The chief replied in surprise, "Who were all those men you had with you there?" The missionary answered, "There were no men there, just my wife and me." The chief argued that they had seen many men standing guard—hundreds of big men in shining garments with drawn swords in their hands.[22] King David described what really goes on behind the scenes: "The angel of the Lord encamps around those who fear him, and he delivers them" (Ps. 34:7). This was Daniel's testimony too, who witnessed first hand the powerful presence of guardian angels when he spent that harrowing night alone in the lions' den (Dan. 6:22).

Angels are also assigned to fight alongside us in this spiritual war. Daniel saw the Ancient of Days going into battle with thousands upon thousands attending him and ten thousand times ten thousand standing before him (Dan. 7:10). And Joel refers to these "heavenly beings" (Ps. 29:1) or "mighty ones" (Ps. 103:20) when he prays, "Bring down your warriors, O Lord" (Joel 3:11), and Deborah too when she proclaimed, "From heaven the stars fought, from their courses they fought against Sisera" (Judg. 5:20).

According to some scholars, these same warriors, depicted as the "starry host," are called into military file "one by one" (Isa. 40:26 NIV). This spiritual army is also depicted in an otherwise cryptic piece of military instruction the Lord gave to David as he was about to attack the Philistines, "You shall not go up; go around to their rear, and come against them opposite the balsam trees. And when you hear the sound of marching in the tops of the balsam trees, then rouse yourself, for the Lord has gone out before you to strike down the army of the Philistines" (2 Sam. 5:23-24).

The battle between the Israelites and the Philistines was more than just a physical conflict. "Marching in the tops of the balsam trees" was "an army of God" (1 Chron. 12:22), and his legions of "mighty ones," were fighting on David's behalf. The passage also suggests evil spiritual warriors were fighting on the side of the Philistines.[23]

SPIRITUAL FORCES OF EVIL IN THE NATURAL WORLD

In addition to influencing people, the New Testament describes a direct connection between spiritual forces of evil and the destructive forces of nature. One such example is the account of the Sea of Galilee crossing when Jesus and his disciples were engulfed in a violent storm. The disciples feared for their lives, but when they searched for Jesus, they found him fast asleep in the back of the boat. When they woke him, he spoke to the wind and waves: "'Peace! Be still!' And the wind ceased, and there was a great calm" (Mark 4:39).

Jesus' "rebuke" is identical to the exorcism narratives found throughout the Gospels, in fact, he used the very same word. *Phimoō, which is* translated "be still," means to "muzzle" or "strangle" something. Both Mark and Luke thematically begin their accounts of Jesus' work on earth by using *this* word when referring to his ministry of deliverance (Mark 1:25; Luke 4:35). It appears, therefore, that Jesus looked upon this seemingly ordinary storm at sea, this ordinary event of nature, as a demonic force, and he strangled it.[24]

Considering this, if spiritual forces of evil have some degree of control over nature, is it too far-fetched to think *they* might be the source of some of the "natural" disasters on earth? This was certainly the case in the life of Job. His friends assumed it was God who sent the tornado that destroyed his property and killed his children (Job 1:19). But it wasn't God, it was Satan. Thankfully, we are told that one day, when the powers of darkness are finally defeated, all natural disasters will cease on the earth (Rev. 21:4).

DEMONS

Hell is empty and all the devils are here—William Shakespeare

The third echelon of power in the Kingdom of Darkness is the demonic realm. Demons are different from territorial spirits in that they seek to live within physical entities rather than in larger geographical regions. Henry Kelley describes them as "parasitic" in nature, which makes sense when we consider how they begged Jesus to let them go into the pigs if they were not allowed to stay in the man[25] (Mark 5:12).

They will sometimes attach themselves to physical objects, like amulets, figurines, or wooden carving, which gives them permission to attack the person who has them in their possession. You've got to be careful what you buy, or wear, or bring into your home, because you might be getting a lot more than you bargained for. God warned his people not to bring the graven images of the Canaanite gods into their homes, or they would suffer the same fate (Deut. 7:26).

We experienced this first-hand several years ago when one of our staff was sick. Nothing seemed to help, but when she prayed, the Lord kept bringing back to her mind some jewelry her maternal grandmother had passed on to her. She knew her grandmother had delved into witchcraft, but never thought too much about it. She was also hesitant to get rid of the jewelry because of her love for her grandma. But the Holy Spirit kept speaking to her. Finally, she disposed of it and within a few days, all her physical ailments disappeared.

Accursed physical objects create a spiritual connection between the people who own them and the supernatural realm. If you're not careful, you could be opening a door that will be difficult to shut. In his book, *Drumming at the Edge of Magic: A Journey into the Spirit of Percussion,* Mickey Hart, former drummer of the "Grateful Dead," talks about the history of the drum from a spiritualistic perspective. He describes Tibetan ritual drums called *damarus,* which are usually made of human skulls. "In 20 years of drum collecting," he says, "I've possessed only two *damarus* … and the first one nearly killed me."

A friend, who bought the drum in India, gave it to Hart, knowing he would appreciate it. When he finally pulled it down from the shelf to give it a few thumps, he was disappointed by its boring sound. "I never expected to play it again," he writes. He set it back on a shelf and then went and threw up. He had no reason to associate his nausea with the *damaru,* but then, he started bumping into things and falling down and injuring himself in minor but annoying ways. "It began to feel as if everything in my life was beginning to unravel," he said. Hart decided to get rid of the drum, returning it to the Tibetan Buddhist center in Berkeley, California. "So you've come home at last," the head Lama said, looking at the drum. Then he turned to Hart, "I hope you have been most careful, Mr. Hart. This is a drum of great, great power. It wakes the dead, you know."[26]

HOW DEMONS TORMENT PEOPLE

Those tormented by evil spirits usually live with a great deal of physical and emotional pain, Greg Boyd observes:

"Blindness, deafness, muteness and deformities are not always mere ailments. They are evidences of a spiritual regime at odds with God's purposes. So too is spiritual blindness (2 Cor. 4:4), hindrances in ministry and evangelism (1 Thes. 2:18), delays in prayer (Dan. 10:1-13), the behavior of evil people (John 13:2), temptation and discouragement (1 Tim. 3:7; 2 Tim. 2:25-26), the struggle with 'strongholds' (2 Cor. 10:3-5), false and legalistic religious teachings (1 Tim. 4:1-4), persecutions (Rev. 2:10), life-threatening 'natural' phenomenon (Mark 4:39), and even death"[27] (Heb. 2:14).

Demons lure people into the bondage of perverted sexual practices, like Mary Magdalene, from whom Jesus cast out seven evil spirits (Luke 8:2). Prostitution has been around for thousands of years, but pornographic literature, films, and videos are a more recent way demons draw people into their web of entrapment and bondage.

They will sometimes cause their victims to experience moments of intense pain, like the man who started screaming in the synagogue (Mark 1:23). I witnessed this in a meeting I was attending several years ago. Out of nowhere, a young woman fell to the ground and began screaming uncontrollably. Every time the name of Jesus was mentioned, she would put her hands over her ears and start to scream again. Finally, some people carried her to another room and she eventually calmed down.

Some physical diseases come from demons too, like the woman Jesus healed of scoliosis. He explained that it was *a spirit* that had been crippling her for eighteen years (Luke 13:11). Many times the Gospels state that Jesus healed a demonized person yet never says anything about exorcism (Matt. 12:22; Matt. 4:24; Luke 7:21). J. Ramsey Michaels surmises it was probably because the line between possession and disease had become so blurred at that point that New Testament authors began to categorize them together.[28] A good example of this is Mark 1:32-34, which mentions the sick and those possessed by demons, whereas the parallel passages in Matthew and Luke refer only to people possessed by demons. All of this begins to make sense when we consider Peter summarized Jesus' ministry by saying, "He went about doing good and healing all who were oppressed by the devil…" (Acts 10:38b).

Another way demons torment people is through nightmares. This was something my wife and I discovered first hand when we were with YWAM Los Angeles. Our fall Discipleship Training School was always our largest school of the year, and one particular year, it was larger than it had ever been before, so much so, that we could not accommodate everyone at our main center in the San Fernando Valley. Fortunately, we found housing at a recently vacated dormitory on the other side of town. After signing the lease agreement, we moved in.

By Monday morning, every room was spick and span as students started arriving from around the world for their five-month intensive. That night was miserable. Almost everyone, staff and students, had terrible nightmares. The following evening, it was more of the same. What was going on? We did some research and discovered a cult had been renting those dorms and moved out a few weeks earlier. Evidently some of the demons were still there. The next morning, we went through every room, singing praise songs and taking authority over the powers of darkness. Nobody experienced nightmares from that point onward.

Perhaps even more difficult to understand than the problem of demonically inspired nightmares, is the idea that schizophrenia can also be demonic. Demons have personalities too, which means that a demonized person has more than one personality living inside of them. In reality, they are not schizophrenic, but what Henry Halley describes as a case of "invaded personality."[29] The Gadarene demoniac, for example, acted and spoke as someone controlled by another person. "What have you to do with us, O Son of God?" they shouted. "Have you come here to torment us before the time?" (Matt. 8:29).

A secular psychiatrist might diagnose such a person with "Dissociative Identity Disorder" (DID), formally known as "Multiple Personality Disorder" (MPD), but where they miss the mark is they see it only as a mental condition. Yes, there are those who are mentally ill, but there is also a spiritual condition that looks very similar and often goes undiagnosed. Unfortunately, the medical community has no clear consensus on diagnostic criteria or treatment because they often leave out the spiritual component from their diagnosis.

And finally, there is an important element in all of this we cannot afford to miss: Jesus' showed great compassion to those tormented by evil spirits. He loved them and wanted to see them set free from their misery. He expressed deep anger toward the self-righteousness of the Pharisees, yet never suggested they were demonized. On the other hand, he was never angry with those possessed by evil spirits but treated them as victims[30] (Mark 5:19).

ACTIVITIES THAT EXPOSE PEOPLE TO DEMONS

Certain activities put people at a greater risk of demonic activity in their lives. Demons are not free to do whatever they please. They live within boundaries of authority, and thus, are only capable of invading a person's mind and heart to the degree they are *given* that authority. For our purpose we will summarize five of the primary activities that expose people to the demonic realm:

- When a person engages in habitual sin, it opens them up to the demonic realm. It is not automatic of course, because there are only a limited number of demons in existence, but if demons are in close proximity to the person committing these sins, it *gives* them an opportunity to gain a foothold in their life.

- Others experience the presence of demons following a traumatic experience. It could be a crime that was committed against them, or the loss of a loved one, or a spirit of fear that came from a vehicle accident. Recording artist, Stormie Omartian, describes her struggle with depression and suicidal thoughts, which came from being locked in a closet as a child by her mentally ill mother. "I would wake up every morning thinking about committing suicide," she says. "It was something I couldn't break." The suicidal thoughts continued into her adult life, and didn't stop until her pastor's wife prayer prayed over her. "Suddenly, the spirit's of depression and suicide left," she says. "The next morning I awoke without any feelings of depression whatsoever. No thoughts of suicide, no heaviness in my chest, no fearful anticipation of the future. I waited all day for it to return, but it never did. Day after day it was the same. It's been several years now, and I have never experienced those feelings again, nor the paralysis that came with them!"

- A third link to the demonic realm comes through our parents' or grandparents' involvement in the occult. This was the case in my own life, where I had to break a connection to the demonic realm that came through my grandfather's involvement in Freemasonry. I had no personal involvement with this group, but my grandfathers' association with them had a spiritual impact upon me that needed to be broken.

- Personal involvement in the occult or other forms of paranormal activity will also expose a person to the demonic realm in a very real way. Even if their involvement was casual, it can still affect them for years to come. Some of the most common forms of occult activity today are witchcraft, including various forms of black magic, the use of spells and the invocation of spirits, séances, seeking to contact the dead through a Medium, playing with Ouija boards, fortune telling, crystal balls, palm reading, tea leaf reading, tarot cards, and astrology (not astronomy), which is the belief that the sun, moon, and stars are "gods" who rule over us.

- Drug use can also open a person to the demonic realm. In the New Testament the word is *pharmakōn,* from which comes our English word *pharmacy*. It describes a religious experience through the use of chemicals, which diminishes a person's capacity to control what comes in and out of their minds and hearts. This is why *pharmakōn* is linked to *sorcery* in the New Testament (Rev. 9:21).

Matthew Murray used drugs and had a morbid obsession with death and paranormal activity. "I'm going to sleep with the dead people," he told the other kids who were with him at an old church during a youth retreat. He then made his way up into the attic to sleep for the night. When he came to DTS he started exhibiting the same type of strange behavior, eventually diving headfirst into an exploration of the occult.

PERSONAL APPLICATION

It is not dangerous to know all the Bible teaches us about the enemy; it is dangerous to remain ignorant—Dean Sherman

Jesus sent out the disciples to preach the gospel *and* cast out demons (Mark 3:14-15). Right away we meet something very peculiar in his Great Commission mandate. Evangelism and spiritual warfare were meant to go hand in hand. How did we miss that? When we share our faith without first taking authority over the powers of darkness we end up with mixed results. "How can someone enter a strong man's house and plunder his goods," Jesus asked, "unless he first binds the strong man? Then indeed he may plunder his house." (Matt. 12:29). So what about you?

Have you tried to share your faith without taking authority over the powers of darkness? What happened?

It's naive to think Satan is going to allow us carry off his possessions without putting up a struggle. There's a lot at stake for him, especially when the people we are trying to reach have the potential to do great things for God. The intensity of the battle also depends on the location. Let's not forget that Jesus sends us into "all" the world. This includes the darkest and most corrupt places on earth. These are the strongholds of the enemy—their house. And we're not just talking about dark places in distant lands. Demonic strongholds are alive and well in our own backyard—in our schools, political and financial institutions, and our places of employment. Jesus' implication here is that we cannot effectively impact these spheres of society, let alone other nations, until we first tie up the strong man.

To make this possible God clothes us with spiritual armor (Eph. 6:13), and equips us with spiritual weapons powerful enough to destroy the devil's strongholds (2 Cor. 10:4). More importantly still, he is with us every step of the way. At the heart of Jesus' commission stands an unchanging message of hope: "I am with you always" (Mt. 28:20).

Is the battle you are fighting God's battle?

Before we do anything else, we need to make sure the battle we are fighting is God's battle, not just our own. In case we missed the point, our adversary is a lot more powerful than we are, so engaging him in our own strength is definitely a recipe for disaster. "Be strong *in the Lord* and in the power of *his* might," the Bible instructs us (Eph. 6:10).

David knew God was on his side when he stepped onto that deserted battlefield to face the champion of the Philistines. All the other soldiers had retreated (1 Sam. 17:24), and he was all alone, except for one key factor: God was with him! For years I saw this as a battle between two human beings, David and Goliath, when in reality, it was a battle between their gods. This was *spiritual* warfare at the highest level. "Am I a dog, that you come at me with sticks?" Goliath scoffed at him. Then he cursed David by his gods (1 Sam. 17:43). David's response gives us God's blueprint for defeating spiritual giants in our own lives: "I come to you in the name of the Lord of hosts, the God of the armies of Israel, whom you have defied" he said (1 Sam. 17:45). And that is the question we must ask ourselves: Is the battle we are fighting the Lord's battle or just our own?

What weapon has God placed in your hand?

Saul tried to clothe David with his own armor (1 Sam. 17:38-39), but it didn't fit. Saul was a grown man, and David, just a teenager. He knew he would fail if he tried to wear that bulky armor, so he took it off. "I can't fight in this," he said to Saul. He decided to go with what he knew best. His slingshot. No one had ever defeated a giant with a slingshot before but David knew this was the right weapon for him. He had stopped a lion and a bear this way, and he was confident he could do it again. What has God placed in your hand? Don't worry if it's unconventional or different. Use what God has given to you and you will be victorious.

CHAPTER EIGHT

Divine testing

God does not willingly bring affliction or grief to anyone.

—JEREMIAH

Now we arrive at what is, without question, the most difficult area of suffering to understand: God. Does God cause suffering? It's one of the main questions people ask, and the simple answer is, yes, he does, but it's not what many of them think. We are told he does not *willingly* bring affliction or grief to anyone (Lam. 3:33), but yes, he allows, and even causes suffering in certain instances. In the next three chapters we will explore the reasons suffering comes, directly or indirectly, from the hand of God. The first is divine testing.

God tests those who belong to him. He is described as a master gardener who prunes the trees in his garden to make them more fruitful (John 15:1-2). Because he loves us, he cuts away dead and wayward branches in our lives. He has a picture of what he wants us to look like in the end, but to get there he must trim back the growth that is going in the wrong direction.

The writer of Hebrews tells us God disciplines the ones he loves. This is the word *paideuó* in Greek, which means: To train someone to go in the right direction. Coincidentally, training is the same word horticulturalists use to describe the physical act of pruning. He (or she[1]) explains that God does this because we are his children. If we were not his, he wouldn't feel the same need to make us into better people (Heb. 12:6-7).

GOD'S MOTIVE IS ALWAYS TO BLESS US

The New Testament meets us from time to time with complex statements that demand a more in-depth explanation. James Chapter 1 is one such instance. It says God "tempts no one," which would seem to indicate the testing of our faith never comes from him. But there's more to this passage than what meets the eye. The word tempt is *peirazó,* which can mean *either* test or tempt, depending on the context of the passage. Sometimes it is used in the negative sense, like in verse 13, but at other times, it appears in the positive sense, like in verse 12: "Blessed is the man who remains steadfast under trial (peirazó) for when he has stood the test he will receive the crown of life, which God has promised to those who love him."

So, does God test us? Yes, but it's never in the negative sense, to bring us down, but always in the positive sense, to build us up. Bible scholar Matthew Henry says that afflictions, as sent by God, are designed to draw out our graces, not our corruptions. And Lutheran pastor R.C.H. Lenski agrees, pointing out that when Paul penned, "examine (peirazó) yourselves to see whether you are in the faith" (2 Cor. 13:5), he did not mean to "tempt" yourself but rather, "prove" yourself. "Testing oneself is simple enough," he says. "A few honest questions honestly answered soon reveal where one stands."[2]

TESTING IS A SIGN GOD CAN TRUST US

Another issue relates to the recently popular notion that serving God would never include suffering of any kind. "Such a theology," Yancey contends, "could only spring up in times of affluence, in a society well stocked with pain-relieving aids. Christians in Iran, say, or China could hardly come up with such a smiley-face theology."[3]

Reflecting this truth, one Eastern European Christian observed, "You Western Christians often seem to consider material prosperity to be the only sign of God's blessing. On the other hand, you often seem to perceive poverty, discomfort, and suffering as signs of God's disfavor. In some ways we in the East understand suffering from the opposite perspective. We believe that suffering may be a sign of God's favor and trust in the Christians to whom the trial is permitted to come."[4]

Wow, what a different take on things. God allows us to be tested because he knows we can handle it, but even when he does this, as the apostle Paul pointed out, he will never allow it to go beyond our ability (1 Cor. 10:13).

SOME OF GOD'S WAYS IN TESTING

Fruitfulness is one of the primary evidences of God's presence in our lives. The book of Galatians mentions nine of them: "Love, joy, peace, patience, kindness, goodness, faithfulness, gentleness and self-control" (Gal. 5:22-23). As we have glimpsed, God's pruning is necessary to bring them forth in our lives. Vineyard workers will sometimes cut back as much as 90% of old growth to produce the greatest amount of fruitfulness the following year. It's in these times of pruning, we could easily imagine God is angry with us, when, in reality, he is simply preparing us for greater fruitfulness.

This was the case with King Hezekiah when God withdrew from him, "in order to test him and to know all that was in his heart" (2 Chron. 32:31). Pastor Rick Warren points out that up until that point, Hezekiah had enjoyed an intimate friendship with God, but at this crucial point in his reign, God withdrew himself to test his character, to reveal his weakness, and prepare him for greater responsibility to come. "Sometimes God intentionally draws back so we don't sense his closeness," he says, "but these incidents, even the smallest ones, have significance for our character development."[5]

God's goal is that we become men and women of strong moral character, whose lives exhibit the fruit of the Spirit in everything we do. In addition to the nine fruit of Galatians, the New Testament mentions others, among them humility, insight, faith, and obedience.

Humility was what God brought forth in the life of Paul, by giving him a thorn in the flesh to keep him from becoming proud. The Bible doesn't tell us what the thorn was, just that Satan was the one causing it. And when Paul asked God to take it away, God simply said that his grace was sufficient, and that his power was made perfect in weakness (2 Cor. 12:9). God could have removed Paul's thorn in the flesh, but he saw it as an opportunity to bring greater humility into his life.

Job went from having secondhand information about God to having a firsthand revelation of him. This insight into God's character was also brought forth through testing. Toward the end of his trials he exclaimed, "I had heard of you by the hearing of the ear, but now my eye sees you" (Job 42:5). Why is it so easy for us to assume God is punishing us when something bad happens? It's human nature to think this way. In a survey of 139 tribal groups from around the world, all but four of them perceived illness as a sign of God's (or the gods') disapproval."[6] This is what Job's counselors had assumed too. *You must have done something wrong, Job, to deserve all of this,* they said. It turns out they were wrong. God wasn't judging him at all. He was only testing him!

Faith is unwavering confidence in God. Abraham believed God would keep his promise to give him descendants, even though everything in the natural suggested otherwise. God had required that he sacrifice his son on the altar. It was the ultimate test of his faith, yet Abraham never wavered. He knew God would keep his promise, even if it meant he would have to bring his son back from the dead (Heb. 11:19).

And finally, **obedience**, that even Jesus learned through the things he suffered (Heb. 5:8). It wasn't that he had to learn something he didn't already know, but rather, he brought to completion that which was still unresolved in the plans and purposes of God. The word "learned" in this passage is *emathen* from which comes our English word *math*. In other words, there was a problem that needed to be solved, and the way God chose to solve it was through Jesus' obedience to die on the cross (Phil. 2:8).

C.S. Lewis says he believes God will even use evil people to produce what he called, "the complex good" in our lives.[7] This was certainly the case with Moses and Jesus, who were persecuted by evil men who tried to kill them. And David too, whose refinement came at the hands of a mad king who threw spears at him and constantly looked for an opportunity to take his life.[8] After many years Joseph finally understood this too. "You meant evil against me," he said to his brothers, who had sold him into a life of slavery. "But God meant it for good" (Gen. 50:20).

LEADERS FACE THE GREATEST AMOUNT OF GOD'S TESTING

God tests leaders because this is what qualifies them to lead others. But it's not a quick or easy process. Moses spent 40 years in obscurity before he was ready to be the leader of God's people. So too, King David, who had the first inkling of God's calling on his life when he was barely 13 years old, but it took another decade and a half before he would finally ascend to the throne.

It is during the season of testing we learn to minister to others. In the words of Mother Teresa, "One must have suffered oneself to help others." She was right. God's pathway takes leaders through deep and dark valleys, where God guides them, and comforts them, and teaches them his ways (Ps. 23:4). The point we cannot afford to miss is that the entire process is on purpose. This is our teachable moment, the place where we learn to comfort others with *the same comfort* we received from God. (2 Cor. 1:4).

Leaders face the greatest amount of opposition to their ideas and vision. Think of Martin Luther King Jr. His life changed an entire nation. "What doesn't destroy me makes me stronger," he said. He accepted beatings, jailings, and other brutalities because he knew a complacent nation would only rally behind his cause if they saw the evil of racism in its ugliest form. And they did. The pain he walked through paved the way for millions of black Americans to experience a level of freedom he never experienced himself. Like Queen Esther before him, he understood his place in history (Est. 4:14). I love the way Sir Paul McCartney put it in one of his songs: "Blackbird singing in the dead of night. Take these broken wings and learn to fly. All your life, you were only waiting for this moment to arise."[9]

"Christianity," King observed, "has always insisted that the cross we bear should precede the crown we wear. To be a Christian," he said, "one must take up his cross, with all its difficulties and agonizing, tension-packed content, and carry it until that very cross leaves its mark upon us and redeems us to that more excellent way which comes only through suffering."[10]

NOT ALL TESTING COMES FROM GOD

People who have endured a lifetime of physical disability often assume their suffering is the testing of God. As we saw in Chapter Three, we *all* suffer physically because of The Fall. Some people more than others. One such person is highlighted in the story of the man born blind in John Chapter 9. The text gives the impression God had purposely allowed this man to be born without sight so God could be glorified when Jesus healed him. The problem, however, is that John 3:16 says God loves *every* human being unconditionally. Why, then, would he allow this man to endure years of suffering simply so God could receive the glory? That would be the height of selfishness on God's behalf, wouldn't it? But that is what the passage seems to say.

The NASB reads like this, "Jesus answered, '*It was* neither that this man sinned, nor his parents; *but it was so that* the works of God might be displayed in him. We must work the works of Him who sent me as long as it is day; night is coming when no one can work'" (John 9:3-4).

The passage indicates the man was born blind so Jesus could be glorified through his healing, but a closer look tells a very different story. The early Greek manuscripts were written in all capital letters. Most had no punctuation except for paragraph breaks, and there were no spaces between words. Because of this, the spaces, accents, breathing marks, and punctuation had to be supplied by the translator. Most of the time these additions are helpful, but in some instances the translation is influenced by the presuppositions of the translator.

In John Chapter 9, the Greek words '*it was,*' '*that,*' and '*it was*' are simply not there. That is why they are in italics in the NASB. If you read the text as the Greek reads, without the additional English words, you can see that the question is answered first, and then, Jesus goes on with his original business of healing the man."[11]

A better way for this passage to be translated is:

"Jesus answered, 'neither this man sinned, nor his parents. But so that the works of God might be displayed in him, we must work the works of Him who sent me as long as it is day; night is coming when no one can work'" (John 9:3-4).

In other words, "Stop asking these ridiculous questions about whose fault it was. That's not important. What we need to do is get on with the work God called me to do because we don't have much time left." Basically, Jesus never explained *why* the man was born blind, he only said it was *not* because of sin. And even more importantly, he *did not* say it was God who caused his blindness so he could be glorified in his healing.

PERSONAL APPLICATION

In what ways have you experienced the testing of God in your life?

God's testing comes in many shapes and forms. Paul experienced it as a thorn in his flesh, Job got sick and lost his possessions, and the Children of Israel had to deal with the Canaanites God had left in the Promised Land (Judg. 3:1). In what ways has God tested you? Your response must be to look at it as a privilege, as James explained to the Jewish believers scattered across Palestine because of persecution: "The testing of your faith," he said, "produces steadfastness" (James 1:3).

Have you seen testing as punishment or as God's loving hand?

When testing comes, we should not assume it is because we have done something wrong. Every great man or woman of

God will be tested to one degree or another. It is a sign that we belong to him: "For the Lord disciplines the one he loves, and chastises every son whom he receives" (Heb. 12:6). Just let God strip away the dead branches, let him prune and train you, and then, let him mold you into the image he has always envisioned for your life.

CHAPTER NINE

God's judgment on sin

"God's ultimate end in all that he does ... is the highest well-being of himself and of his universe."

—CHARLES FINNEY

Faced with the problem of man's sin, God had a moral dilemma. He loved man and didn't want to see him die, but because he is just, he couldn't ignore man's rebellion altogether. Death was the consequence for sin, summed up in the words of the prophet Ezekiel, "The soul who sins shall die" (Ezek. 18:20), and the apostle Paul, "The wages of sin is death" (Rom. 6:23). There was no easy way for God to get around the legal requirements of his own law. He didn't want to see man die, but he had to do the right thing or he would be in violation of his own moral character.

While my understanding of justice is perfectly consistent with the culture in which I live, God's perspective is sometimes different. He never exercises one aspect of his character if it compromises another. This meant that if God wanted to extend mercy to man he had to find a way to do so without compromising his law.

Before we go any further, it's important for us to understand that what looks like God's judgment is sometimes his withdrawal from the situation, allowing people to experience the natural consequence of their sin. For example, the Old Testament does not have a specific word for punishment.[1] *Paqad*, which is usually translated "to punish," is better translated "to visit." So when God says, "Shall I not punish them for these things?" (Jer. 5:9), his intent is that their own wickedness would be visited upon them. Old Testament scholar Klaus Koch tells us the phrase usually translated "retaliate" or "pay back" actually means "bringing to completion."[2] In other words, sinners receive the punishment for their sin when it is allowed to be brought to full completion. The book of James reflects this same perspective when it says, "But each person is tempted when he is lured and enticed by his own desire" (Jas. 1:14).

Let's not forget, however, that regardless of how the judgment comes, God hates it when we suffer because of our sin. His ultimate intent is to be gracious to us and show us compassion (Isa. 30:18). But what happens if someone ignores his warnings and stubbornly continues to do what they know is wrong? What is God supposed to do? His only viable option is to allow them to face the consequences of their actions. Is he unjust for doing so? Is he unloving? No, he is simply doing what he *must* do. People blame him when they suffer because of their sin, but is God really to blame?

"If a man is incarcerated for stealing a car, whose fault is it that he is in prison? Do we say it is the judge's fault? No, the man himself bears the full responsibility for his actions, even though it was the judge who sentenced him. More to the point, if the prisoner's daughter misses her father because he is in prison, is it the judge's fault the girl is separated from her dad?

No, it's the criminal's fault. The child's grief is a consequence of her father's crime. Innocent people are often affected by a judge's sentencing of a guilty party, but in neither case is the suffering the responsibility of the judge."[3]

One might argue that if God were truly loving he would find a way to eliminate every form of punishment altogether. Wouldn't that be the most loving thing for him to do? Apparently not. The Bible tells us that when people are not held accountable for their sin, their hearts become *filled* with schemes to do wrong (Eccles. 8:11).

Following are four ways God has carried out his judgment on the human race. Remember, it is always his last resort. His habit is to warn people ahead of time, usually through prophetic voices, but when all else fails, he *must* do the right thing. His commitment to justice demands it.

GOD'S JUDGMENT THROUGH NATURE

Throughout history God has used natural disasters as a means of judging people for their sin. We read of earthquakes (Num. 16:32) and droughts (2 Chron. 7:13), and one occasion, meteorites that rained down fire from heaven to destroy an evil city (Gen. 19:24). Of course, the most destructive of all of God's judgments was a flood that engulfed the earth (Gen. 7:11-12). Some suggest the flood narrative is better interpreted as God's rescue plan of the human race rather than his punishment on sin, but either way, God used the forces of nature to deal with the sin that had become rampant on the earth.

The Flood narrative is prefaced by the curious account of 'the sons of God' entering into an unnatural sexual union with 'the daughters of man' and begetting hybrid beings known as the Nephilim (Gen. 6:1-4). The reason the author uses this story to preface the Flood account is to explain why God had to start over with his plans for humans and the world. Not only had man sunk to the point that, "every intention of the thoughts of his heart was only evil continually" (Gen. 6:5), but the unnatural union of fallen angelic beings and human women was corrupting God's creative order in which everything was to reproduce according to their own kind (Gen. 1:21, 24-25).

More importantly, the introduction of the hybrid Nephilim was corrupting the human gene pool, which meant God's plans for humans to reflect his image and his loving rule over the earth and animals was in jeopardy. This might explain why God went to such an extreme of withdrawing his Spirit and allowing forces of destruction to revert creation back to a "formless and void" state. "While the Flood was a grievous judgment on the world," Greg Boyd says, "it was even more fundamentally *a rescue operation*. Only by going to this extreme could God preserve his dream for eventually uniting himself to humans and inviting them to share in his triune love and rule forever."[4]

Should we fear God's judgment? Absolutely. The Bible tells us to fear him. Not just once or twice, but almost two hundred times! In several instances, the word "fear" is the word "respect" or "reverence" for God, but in some cases it is the word "terror" (*phobeó*). One example is when Jesus cautioned the disciples to fear God more than what human authorities were capable of doing to them (Matt. 10:28).

At any moment God could, once again, use the physical creation as an instrument of his judgment upon the earth. I think we are more vulnerable than people realize. If 70% of life on earth was extinguished when a meteor struck the Yucatán Peninsula, triggering what scientists describe as an "impact winter," couldn't it happen again? If everything is held together by God (Col. 1:17), all he has to do is loosen his grasp a little bit and everything would quickly begin to unravel.

An equally frightening possibility is a direct hit from a magnetar. Magnetars happen when stars run out of nuclear fuel and collapse under their own weight. The result is a super-nova, the largest explosion we know of in the universe. This spectacular stellar death leaves behind a neutron star, which usually burns out on its own, but a small number of them become magnetars, which fire massive x-ray and gamma ray flashes across the universe. Regardless of the distance, they can destroy anything in their path. A direct hit from a magnetar would immediately extinguish all life on earth says Peter Tuthill of Sydney University in Australia. And astrophysicist Adrian Melott of the University of Kansas agrees. "A scenario is conceivable in which an extremely powerful gamma ray burst could strike us and instantaneously evaporate 25% of the ozone layer. "That would be very bad."[5]

Let's remember, however, that the vast majority of earthquakes, droughts, and other natural disasters have nothing to do with God. They are simply the result of a planet in the final stages of decay and self-destruction, but there is no denying sometimes these catastrophic events are, indeed, acts of God.

GOD'S JUDGMENT THROUGH ANGELS

The most well-known account of God's judgment through an angel is the story of Passover in Egypt, but there are others. On one occasion, an angel wiped out an entire army in a single night (2 Kings 19:35). In another instance it was Israel's turn. Remember, God is no respecter of persons. His standards are the same for everyone, whether they call themselves by his name or not. In Israel's case it was because of King David's sin. When David realized *he* was the reason for the judgment of God, he fell facedown and cried out for mercy (1 Chron. 21:16). And God listened. "It is enough," he said to the angel. "Now stay your hand" (2 Sam. 24:16). A New Testament example is when an angel killed King Herod because of his sin. Unlike David, he refused to humble himself before God (Acts 12:23).

GOD'S JUDGMENT THROUGH EVIL SPIRITS

God will sometimes use demonic spirits to judge evil people for their sin. The description of these occurrences is infrequent, five of them in all, but it is clear the judgment is from God:

- God used an evil spirit to stir up civic unrest among the people of Shechem (Judg. 9:22-25)

- God sent an evil spirit that caused Saul to act erratically, a behavior that eventually led to his downfall as king (1 Sam. 16:14).

- God assigned a lying spirit to influence Ahab to go to war against Ramoth-Gilead, which resulted in his death (1 Kings 22:20-23).

- God sent a spirit of confusion to come upon the Egyptians (Isa. 19:14).

- God directed a spirit to persuade Sennacherib to return to his homeland in Nineveh, where he was assassinated by two of his sons (Isa. 37:38).

As a result of these passages, some suggest God is the author of both good and evil. They cite Isaiah 45:7, "I form light and create darkness; I make well-being and create calamity," and Lamentations 3:38, "Is it not from the mouth of the Most High that good and bad come?" But these scriptures are taken out of context. For example, in Isaiah 45:7, the subject matter relates to the future deliverance of the children of Israel from Babylon, hence the "light and darkness" of this passage relates to "liberation and captivity" and the "well-being and calamity" refer to God's plans to bless Israel and curse Babylon.

In Lamentations 3:38, the writer asks, "Is it not from the mouth of the Most High that good and bad come?" Taken out of context, and made into a stand-alone statement, this verse could, indeed, support the idea that both good and evil come from the Lord. If read, however, in its context, it says nothing of the sort. The preceding verse (Lam. 3:37) indicates that the subject matter of the verse concerns a specific prophecy. Israel had been warned that calamity was about to come upon them because of their unloving behavior toward their fellow man. In the verses preceding verse 37, the prophet warns them, "If people crush underfoot all the prisoners of the land, if they deprive others of their rights in defiance of the Most High, if they twist justice in the courts—doesn't the Lord see all these things?" (Lam. 3:34-36 NLT).

In other words, the Lord had seen the injustice of Israel and had prophetically warned them to change their ways. Most ignored the prophecy, wanting only to believe prophetic words that announced "good things." However, when calamity did strike, they blamed it on God! In response, Jeremiah reminded them of their sin and the warning that had come "from the mouth of the Most High."[6] God's decision to send calamity or blessing rested solely upon their decision to do right or wrong. If they did what was right, God would bless them, but if they did what was wrong, God would send calamity.

In any case, in response to the question, "Can evil spirits be sent from the Lord?" the answer is yes. Sometimes he will use the destructive power of demonic forces to carry out his judgment on sin.

GOD'S JUDGMENT THROUGH HUMAN BEINGS

When people by their conduct deserve an evil ruler,
God allows such to come forth—Gordon Olson

In the book of Judges, God repeatedly allowed oppressive leaders to rise up and rule over Israel. God wanted them to turn back to him so he could bless them, but when they refused to heed his warnings about their sin, he allowed them to be given over to their enemies. They were sold into the hands of the king of Aram, who ruled over them for eight years, followed by an eighteen-year stretch under the king of Moab. You would think they would have learned their lesson, but instead, they stubbornly continued in their sinful behavior.

That's when the Canaanites arrived. Their commander, Sisera, was an especially ruthless ruler, who oppressed them for close to twenty years. Finally, they turned to God for help, and in his mercy, he delivered them. Deborah, the prophetess-leader of Israel liberated them from Sisera and his Canaanite hordes. But it didn't last long. As soon as they were free again, they went right back to their evil ways. This time God allowed the Midianites to overthrow them, followed by the Philistines and Ammonites. It was basically a case of sowing and reaping. As Galatians 6:7 says, " For whatever one sows, that will he also reap."

I was halfway through my message when a student's hand shot up from the back of the room. "What I don't get is how God could mandate the destruction of whole villages including innocent women and children," he said. "How could anyone in their right mind justify this kind of behavior?" It was a good question and not the first time someone had asked it. It seems every time I talk about God's love and justice, this question comes up. On more than one occasion, God mandated the destruction of every living thing (Deut. 2:34; Josh. 6:21; 1 Sam. 15:3). Like many of you, I have wondered why God would command such harsh and violent behavior. It is not consistent with the character of the God I have come to know.

Some suggest Moses, Joshua and Samuel misunderstood God's instructions, and that he didn't really intend for them to kill anyone, just drive them out. But this seems unlikely, considering all three men received the same instructions from God despite living at different time periods. More plausible is that they heard God correctly, but there is more to the story than what meets the eye. Consider the following five factors:

- First of all, the extermination of the Canaanites had nothing to do with race or ethnicity. God did not command Israel to attack them because they were different, because, in reality, they were Semitic, just like the Israelites. Several of them were actually their distant relatives. The Midianites, for example, traced their ancestry back to Midian, who was one of Abraham's sons (Gen. 25:2). The Amorites, Hivites, and Jebusites, all descended from Ham (Gen. 10:6), and the Moabites and Ammonites were the descendants of Abraham's nephew, Lot (Gen. 19:36-38). Many of them were nomadic peoples, who at one time or another had all lived in Canaan, which is why the Bible refers to them collectively as "The Canaanites." The point we must grasp, however, is that God's command to destroy them was not genocide. It was simply his judgment on people because of their sin.

- Secondly, the Canaanites were not innocent people. They were regularly involved in perverted practices like incest (Gen. 19:31), infant sacrifice (Deut. 12:31), and sex with animals. It is not surprising the Canaanites practiced bestiality, because the god they worshiped also practiced it. From the Canaanite epic poem "The Baal Cycle," we read: "Mightiest Baal hears; He makes love with a heifer in the outback; A cow in the field of Death's Realm."[7] These evil practices were such an abomination to God that on one occasion he confided to his friend Jeremiah that it had never even crossed his mind that they would do such a thing (Jer. 32:35 NLT).

- Because of the level of their sexual depravity, the Canaanites undoubtedly had sexually transmittable diseases which would have been passed on to the Israelites had they brought them into their midst. Their regular engagement in bestiality and child sexual abuse also meant these STDs would have by that time spread throughout the entire population, including the animals and children. Part of God's strategy, it seems, was to limit the spread of these communicable diseases.

- Another important consideration is that God used war in the Old Testament as a means of judging people for their sin, not excluding his own people when they went astray. Some have mistakenly assumed God's wrath was only directed at the Canaanites, and this is simply not true. If an Israelite were to sacrifice his child to Molech, he, too, was to be put to death (Lev. 20:2). The same was true of bestiality (Lev. 20:15), and other sins. When the Israelites began serving other gods, they too came under judgment (1 Kings 14:15). Paul was right in saying there has *never* been favoritism with God (Rom. 2:11).

- Many wonder why the God of the Old Testament seems harsh and judgmental, but then, we find a more merciful and compassionate God when we arrive at the New Testament. The answer, I believe, is the Cross. Jesus' death changed everything! Prior to the Crucifixion, the law required that a person be put to death for their sin, but when Jesus died, God laid *on him* the sins of us all (Isa. 53:6). From that moment forward, God was no longer obligated by his own righteousness to punish sin immediately. Instead, he was able to give people more time to repent without compromising his own integrity. Did he change? No. He is still the same God, committed to doing what is just and right in every situation.

In my view, God is just in everything he does. So what was his motive for mandating the destruction of *every living thing*, including children? The answer must be, can *only* be, that this was the most just and loving thing for him to do.

Consider this: Sin is determined by our *knowledge* of what is right and wrong. James says, "Whoever knows the right thing to do and fails to do it, for him it is sin" (James 4:17). Each of us is responsible to live according to our *personal knowledge* of what is right and wrong. But what if a person *does not fully understand* that what they are doing is wrong? For example, someone who is mentally ill, or a child, whose mind and conscience is not yet fully developed—they do not yet have a full grasp on what is right and wrong in the world. Therefore, they are not fully responsible for their actions. If God requires *more* of those who *know* more (Luke 12:48), doesn't it make sense he would require *less* of those who *know* less?

In short, God was faced with two difficult options: To leave thousands of parentless children living in the land, most of them suffering with venereal disease and sexual trauma, or to bring them immediately into his presence. As innocent children they would have undoubtedly been carried into the presence of God without delay, whereas this would not have been the case if they had continued living on earth. In his foreknowledge God could see the trajectory of their lives following down the same destructive pathway as their parents and grandparents, and decided it would be the most loving thing to bring them home early. God sees everything from an eternal perspective, and in some cases, allows the innocent (*tsaddiq*) to, "die before their time," because he is, "protecting them from the evil to come" (Isa. 57:1 NLT).

CAN THE USE OF DEADLY FORCE BE JUSTIFIED?

On August 6, 1945, President Harry S. Truman gave the order to drop an atomic bomb on the Japanese city of Hiroshima. The blast was equivalent to 15,000 tons of TNT and reduced four square miles of the city to ruins. Some 78,000 people died that day, and another 50,000 were injured or went missing. Three days later, a second bomb was dropped on Nagasaki, killing another 40,000. Within the week, Emperor Hirohito announced his country's unconditional surrender, bringing World War II to an end. When the final body count was tallied, over sixty million people had lost their lives during the six years of that great and horrible war.

Was President Truman's decision the right one, or could there have been a more humane way to end the deadliest conflict this world has ever known? Japan's population was armed and commanded to resist any invasion. If the Allies had invaded, it is likely millions of Japanese would have died, as well as many thousands of Allied troops.

No one will ever know if President Truman's decision was the best one, but it raises an interesting question. Is there ever a time when the use of lethal force is justified? And what about war? Is war always evil, or are there *just* wars? I know these are not easy questions, but the answer holds the key to why God might have authorized the use of lethal force in the Old Testament.

I hate war. I believe most global conflicts are motivated by hatred, power or greed. Cases in point are the genocidal wars in Rwanda, Bosnia and Southeast Asia. They underscore the argument that there are times when the use of force is the only reasonable alternative to mass murder.

The main difference between us, and God, of course, is that he sees the outcome of every decision we could ever make. I am convinced this is what has motivated him, in certain instances, to condone the use of force. In his divine foreknowledge, he sees this as the best remaining solution that will produce the least amount of suffering for the greatest number of people involved.

THE FINAL JUDGMENT

The scriptures reveal that in spite of man's rebellion, God still loves him (John 3:16). He longs for reconciliation with us, like the father in Jesus' story of the lost son, but he would never pressure anyone to come back to him if they are adamantly opposed to it. With great reluctance he prepared a place far away from his presence for those who don't want anything to do with him. He respects their decision, but it is clearly not what he wants. Hell was never created for man to begin with, but for the devil and his angels (Matt. 25:41). "To enter heaven is to become more human than we ever succeeded in being on earth," C.S. Lewis said, "but to enter hell is to be banished from humanity."[8] But what will that "banishment" look like? Will it be a place of unquenchable fire, as the scriptures seem to indicate? (Mark 9:43). I don't believe so.

METAPHORIC ILLUSTRATIONS

I hold that the Bible should always be interpreted literally, unless, of course, it is obvious from the wording or the context that what is being said is metaphorical in nature. King David declared that God is a sun and a shield (Ps. 84:11), but clearly he was only using this imagery to convey that God is one who guides and protects us. Jesus said, "I am the door" (John 10:7), but no one in his right mind would think he was speaking literally. Jesus is not a "door." He only used the word so the people would understand he is *the way* to the Father. Jesus was constantly using metaphors like this, in fact, in his public ministry he never taught *without* using them (Mark 4:34).

Considering this, we have to factor in Jesus' communication style if we are to accurately understand what he said about hell. The main word he used was Gehenna, a landfill on the outskirts of Jerusalem (Matt. 5:22). This was an actual place, a deep, narrow glen on the south side of the city, where people at one time had sacrificed their children to Molech (2 Kings 23:10). Later on, it became the local garbage dump where the bodies of criminals and dead animals were discarded, and where fires were kept burning day and night to consume the waste. I'm sure it reeked with the stench of decaying bodies, and there were worms and maggots crawling around and flies everywhere. It must have been a really nasty place—the ideal backdrop for one of Jesus' metaphoric illustrations. It seems clear to me he compared hell to Gehenna so everyone would understand how horrible the place is going to be.

Additionally, if we were to take all references to the afterlife literally, then heaven will be like living in a jewelry store, with sapphires and emeralds, and streets paved with gold (Rev. 21:19-21). But is that what heaven is going to be like? No. These are just figures of speech used to convey how spectacular the place is going to be. Sandra Richter describes heaven this way: "The paradise that was Eden, and the paradise that is the Holy of Holies, and the coming paradise which the prophets envisioned, are all characterized by this single concept: YHWH is present."[9]

If you ask me, the worst thing about hell is that YHWH will *not* be there. What will life be like when everything that flows from his glorious presence is taken away, and all that is left is Satan, and his hoard of demons and fallen angels? Can anyone blame God for describing it in the most nightmarish way possible? If the horrors we see on earth today reflect what *partial* separation from God is like, what will *total* separation be like?

PERSONAL APPLICATION

Are you engaging in sinful activities that could bring God's judgment upon your life?

God tells us to be holy "for" he is holy, not "as" he is holy (1 Pet. 1:16). It's incredible the difference one word can make. God's holiness is sinless perfection, which none of us could ever achieve. The holiness he wants from you and me, on the other hand, is personal and unique to each one of us. It all depends on our individual knowledge of what is right and wrong. So what about you? Are you engaging in activities you *know* are sinful? Allow God to search your heart, and then confess whatever he shows you. Honest confession is what lifts the weight of guilt from our hearts and minds. "When I refused to confess my sin," King David admitted, "my body wasted away ... Day and night your hand of discipline was heavy on me. My strength evaporated like water in the summer heat. Finally, I confessed all my sins to you and stopped trying to hide my guilt. I said to myself, 'I will confess my rebellion to the Lord.' And you forgave me! All my guilt is gone" (Ps. 32:3-5 NLT).

How has the knowledge that God judges sin affected your relationship with him?

People often struggle to understand how a God of love could punish people for their sins, but as we have glimpsed, because God is just, it is one of the things he must do. If your relationship with him has been tainted by this revelation, tell him you trust him. Don't let the things you *don't know* take away from the things you *do know* about him. God has promised to one day explain everything in detail when we see him face to face (1 Cor. 13:12), but for now, he just wants for us to trust him.

CHAPTER TEN

When God doesn't intervene

*Everything God does is just and fair. He is
the faithful God who does no wrong.*
—MOSES

The question that kept coming up in the days and weeks following the Denver shootings was: Why didn't God prevent Matthew Murray from committing these murders? Certainly, he had the ability to stop him because he is all-powerful. "Doesn't that make him at least partially responsible for what took place?" asked the reporter who showed up at my front door the following morning. He went on, "How could God allow something like this to happen, especially to young people who only wanted to serve him on the mission field?" He was right. God does not always prevent bad things from happening.

This is the reason media mogul Ted Turner says he turned away from his own faith as a young man. When his sister died a painful death, he wrote, "I was taught that God was love and that God was powerful, and I couldn't understand how someone so innocent should be allowed to suffer so."[1]

Why doesn't God intervene? It's the question on the minds of hundreds of people I've met, and the truth is, there are no simple answers. If we are looking for a quick and easy explanation for this complicated issue we are likely to come away disappointed. Despite that fact, there are two important considerations that will help explain why God does not always intervene when bad things happen.

WHEN GOD'S INTERVENTION WOULD REQUIRE A REDESIGN OF MAN'S NATURE

God created man with the ability to make his own decisions in life—this was one of the key components in his "Godlikeness" (Gen. 1:26). It was the primary trait that enabled him to love and be loved, but also, the trait that enabled him to make unloving choices, and therefore, cause others to suffer. As man became more and more reckless with his God-given freedom, God had to make a decision. He could remove his free will altogether, which would immediately put a stop to the suffering he was causing in the world, but that would also take away man's ability to love, which was the main reason he was created. The other option was to leave man's personality intact, but try to motivate him to make right choices through other means—and that is what God decided to do.

In the front lobby of our YWAM campus, I sat across from Julie, one of the students who had been with us during the shootings. "At least we know God is in control." she said. I stared silently at her for a few moments, not knowing how to best respond. It had only been a few days since Philip and Tiffany had died and our whole community was still reeling from the shock of it all. And so was I. I think she must have thought I wasn't listening because she repeated the question again, "In spite of everything, God is still in control, right?"

"Thank you," I responded politely, "but you know … I don't really believe that."

"You can't be serious," she said. "How can you say God is not in control? Don't you believe he is all-powerful?"

I paused for a moment trying to find the right words to answer her. This wasn't the first time someone had bristled at my suggestion that God is *not* controlling everything that happens in the world. But was her opinion of our situation correct? I had no idea. My gut feeling was this was simply the independent act of a human being who had used his God-given gift of freedom to commit an evil act.

"The truth is I agree with you in principle," I said. "I know God is sovereign and all-powerful, and I would never want to take anything away from who he is. It's just that I have a hard time believing *this* is what he wanted for Philip and Tiffany. But just to be clear, I don't think God is incapable of controlling everything, it's just that I don't think he does. There's a huge difference between saying God is *incapable* of doing something, and God *chooses* not to do something."

When our children were young, I would often wrestle with them on the family room floor before dinner. We'd push back the couches and roll around on the carpet. It was usually the three of them against me. Of course, my ulterior motive was to get close and cuddle with them. Those are some of my fondest memories of my children.

I remember one evening when my son pinned me to the carpet. He must have been twelve or thirteen at the time. I just lay there laughing and trying to catch my breath, but for him, it was a big deal. After several seconds, he leapt to his feet, ran into the kitchen, and announced to my wife Linda, "I pinned Dad!" It was a moment of great victory for him. He was a scrawny little guy at the time, and I could have easily escaped his grip. But I didn't because my goal in wrestling with my kids was not to prove I was stronger than they were. It was to be with them and have fun with them.

The real issue is not *who God is* but *what God does*. It's not about his *ability or inability* in a given situation—it's entirely about his *strategy* within that situation. If someone were to say, "God is limited," they are mistaken. No one is capable of limiting God because God is infinite.[2] On the other hand, to say, "God *chose* to limit himself," is very different, because *he* is the one who decided it should be that way.

I know this perspective might bother some, but is it really that far-fetched? If you ask me, to suggest God is controlling every single event is much more radical. If he is in absolute control it means *everything* that takes place on earth is his will. It means God *wants* for some babies to be born deformed, for women to be raped, and for hunger, poverty and wars to persist. If everything is part of the will of God, then God *wanted* Matthew Murray to come to YWAM and commit these murders.

I've discovered, unfortunately, that Julie's worldview is commonplace, even in the Christian world. Whenever people say, "Everything happens for a reason," this is essentially what they are saying. And this perspective works fine, I guess, until you come face-to-face with tragedy and your whole world is turned upside down like it was for us. That's the moment you begin to question if what happened to you was really God's will.

Dean Sherman talks about a friend of his in North Africa who was having a hard time finding volunteers to plant trees in the desert and build water catchments. Though his project would benefit many, the people were hesitant, afraid that it might not be God's will to have trees there.

"Many believe that everything that happens is God's will," Dean says: "*Que sera, sera*—whatever will be, will be. Whenever people say this they are saying that evil is inevitable. Whatever has happened, is happening, and will happen, must be the will of God. But this is not a Christian concept. It is fatalism. Other religions have this fatalistic view of the world and the will of God. They say, 'God's will be done.' No matter what happens, it is the will of God."[3]

How did fatalism creep into the Church of Jesus Christ? It started a long time ago. One of the first to foster the idea was the fifth-century theologian Augustine, who taught that evil and suffering do not really exist but are only small components in the larger scope of God's master plan for the world. "If we could only view evil events from God's transcendent, panoramic, timeless perspective," he wrote, "we would see how these events fit in with the God-ordained harmonious cosmic whole. However horrifying the event may appear to our limited perspective, from God's universal perspective, and in accordance with God's meticulous universally controlling will, the evil event actually contributes to the beauty of the whole."[4]

According to Augustine, nothing is ever left to chance. In his opinion, all events, even the ones we thought *we* were choosing were actually being orchestrated from behind the scenes by God. From what I have seen, it is this perspective that turns more people away from God than any other assumption about him. It was certainly the reason I turned away from him as a teenager, even after growing up in a loving Christian home.

I looked across the coffee table at Julie who was still waiting for me to give her an answer. "Do you know what?" I said, "My security doesn't come from the belief that everything is God's will, it comes from the belief that God is able to work all things together for good for those who love him (Rom. 8:28). He doesn't prevent bad things from happening, but he is actively weaving everything together to make something beautiful in the end—even the bad things. 'All things' includes the bad things too, right? But is he the one causing them? No way."

The big breakthrough came for me when I understood the true meaning of the term "the will of God" in scripture. Roger Forster points out that in the New Testament, there are only two Greek roots from which come the words for God's *will* and God's *plan*. One root is *thélō*, which means *wish, will or desire,* and the other is *boúlomai,* from which come the words *counselor* (Mk. 15:43); *taking advice* (Lk. 14:31); and *plan* (Acts 5:38; 17:20; 27:42-43).[5] This was the "aha moment" for me, because in both cases, *God's will* and *God's plan* can be resisted by man!

William of Ockham, an influential figure in laying the foundation for what would eventually become The Great Reformation, described it this way: "God has absolute power *(agistrat absoluta),* by which he can do anything, but he also has ordained power *(agistrat agistra),* by which he condescends to work within the natural and moral laws he has established."[6]

This means there are some things God has set in place ahead of time, which cannot be changed, like the rise and fall of nations (Dan. 2:21), and the timing of Jesus' return to the earth (Matt. 24:36). They also include his unchanging attitude toward sin and death (2 Pet. 3:9), and promises he has made to individuals throughout history (Heb. 6:17). But there are other occurrences that go against his will, like immoral behavior (1 Thess. 4:3), or when innocent children perish (Matt. 18:14). The Bible is clear God *does not want* these things to happen.

Jesus used both words when he was praying in Gethsemane. "Father," he said, "if you are willing (*boúlomai*), please take this cup of suffering away from me. Yet, may your will (*thélēma*) be done, not mine" (Luke 22:42 NLT). In other words, don't allow my present desire to be delivered from this horrible situation to interfere with your strategic plans for the world.

No human being could ever thwart God's big-picture plans, but they can, if they so choose, remove themselves from his plan for them as individuals. God ordains that the new heaven and the new earth will come to pass. He does not, however, ordain which specific individuals will play a part in it!

How then, are we to take verses like, "Everything I plan will come to pass, for I do whatever I wish?" (Isa. 46:10 NLT), or, "You can make many plans, but the Lord's purpose will prevail" (Prov. 19:21 NLT). If we were to take these passages to mean *every* detail of God's plan will *always* come to pass, it would contradict other passages like Luke 7:30: "But the Pharisees and experts in religious law rejected God's plan (*boulēn*) for them." We must, therefore, take them to refer to the broad outlines of what will be accomplished, rather than details regarding what part each individual will play in them.[7]

King David declared that God's sovereignty rules over all (Ps. 103:19), but he could not have been referring to God's *control* of everything, because moral beings can clearly break God's laws. That's what sin is. David broke them himself, and then wept bitterly when his sin was exposed by the prophet Nathan (2 Sam. 12:13). In other words, if we break God's laws, it does not make his sovereignty ineffective. "The sheriff of a county does not lose his position as sheriff, simply because a county resident broke into a house and stole a television set."[8] God is still sovereign, regardless of what people choose to do. He is still God, as Pastor Bill Johnson puts it. "There's a big difference between saying God is *in control* and God is *in charge*." Clearly God is in charge. He is the sovereign ruler of the universe.

Unfortunately, several versions of the Bible utilize the term *Sovereign Lord* frequently. One of them uses the expression over two hundred times. But the word *sovereign* is not what the original Hebrew manuscripts say. Roger Forster points out that, in fact, the term is not used *even once* in the entire Authorized

Version of the Bible! He goes on, "But this is not to deny that God is indeed King of kings, but the reign of God does not make humans into automatons, nor does it make the spiritual battle a fake in which God is directing both sides."[9]

The actual term that appears hundreds of times in the original language is *Adonai Yahweh,* which translated means *Lord God.*

> "Whatever we understand by the term *Sovereign,*" Forster says, "it cannot be taken to imply that there are no powers but God in the universe. God's rightful dominion is obviously the whole universe, but parts of it are, in practice, usurped by other agents to whom he has given some independence of will and delegated authority."[10]

Human beings fit into this category. One of the first things God did after creating the earth was to entrust man with the responsibility to rule over the rest of his creation (Gen. 1:28). The word God used here is *radah,* which means to take dominion over something. In other words, God gave man the responsibility and authority to steward the earth. It is in this context we can accurately understand the parameters of man's free will.

Free will is the term used to describe God's delegated authority by which he allows man to make decisions independently from himself. In other words, he limits how much control *he* will exercise over man, so man can be in control of his own destiny. This is not a new concept, but one that reflects the view of most of the early church fathers. Consider the following statements made by some of the key spiritual figures in the first three centuries:

• "God, wishing that men and angels follow his will, resolved to create them free." **Justin Martyr**

- "God made man a free agent from the beginning, possessing his own soul to obey the behests of God voluntarily, and not by the compulsion of God." **Irenaeus of Gaul**

- "I find, then, that man was by God constituted free, master of his own will and power ... he sets before man good and evil, life and death, that the entire course of discipline is arranged in precepts by God's calling men from sin, and threatening and exhorting them; and this on no other ground than that man is free, with a will either for obedience or resistance." **Tertullian of Carthage**

- "We were not created to die, but we die by our own fault. Our free-will has destroyed us." **Tatian of Syria**

- "There are, indeed, innumerable passages in the Scriptures which establish with exceeding clearness the existence of freedom of will." **Origen of Alexandria**

- "Those who decide that man is not possessed of free-will, and affirm that he is governed by the unavoidable necessities of fate ... are guilty of impiety toward God himself, making him out to be the cause and author of human evils." **Methodius of Olympus**

- "There is not a class of souls sinning by nature and a class of souls practicing righteousness by nature; but both act from choice." **Cyril of Jerusalem**

The concept of man's free will is one of the foundational cornerstones of the Christian faith. Consider this: Not a single figure in the first 300 years of the Church rejected the concept of man's free will, and most of them stated it clearly in works that are still in existence today.[11]

God has entrusted to every man and woman the freedom to chart the course of his or her own life. It is this decision that at times has caused him a great deal of heartache. It would have been a lot less complicated if he had never given man the free-dom to do whatever he pleases. God would have, in this case, been in complete control of everything that took place on earth, which would mean nothing could ever happen that was contrary to his will. It would mean no one would ever do some-thing that would grieve him (Gen. 6:6), or provoke him to anger (1 Kings 11:9), and he would never regret the way things turned out (1 Sam. 15:35). But that is not what he wanted.

If God had created man this way, theologian Gordon Olson explains, he might have delighted in the profoundness of his operations but could never experience the joy of observing moral creatures that would choose, of their own self-caused volition, to be in happy submission and admiration of his great attributes and moral character.[12] So he created man like him-self, with a mind, emotions, and a free will. It was the only way God could interact with man on an intimate and personal level. "Moral beings must *always* be allowed to be the author of their own actions," Olson says, "or their created 'image' will be rendered inoperative."[13]

To suggest, as some have, that this perspective takes away from the greatness of God, is to miss the point. I would argue the opposite is actually the case. One of the most praiseworthy attributes of the God of the Bible is that he was willing to give up some degree of control, even if this could bring him deep personal grief. "A God willing to make things capable of resist-ing him," C.S. Lewis said, "is the most astonishing and unimaginable of all the feats we attribute to (him)."[14]

What needs to change in our thinking is that there is a dif-ference between God's sovereignty over individuals and his sovereignty over the events of history. This is usually where people get off track. The Bible is full of prophecies, many which have already come to pass. There are 31,173 verses in the Bible, and, according to J. Barton Payne's *Encyclopedia of Biblical*

Prophecy, 8,352 of them are prophetic in nature. This means approximately one out of every four verses in the Bible is prophetic. Prophecy is God's way of saying, "The trajectory of history is going to go in this direction, and I am telling you about it ahead of time so you will know I am God when it comes to pass."

Sometimes God prevents certain things from happening because they are getting in the way of his big-picture plans for the world. The word "lest" means: *So as to prevent something else from happening.* For example, I might say, "I'm going to fill up my car at the service station this morning *lest* I run out of fuel on my way home from work." Or, "I'm not going to take a nap this afternoon *lest* I lie awake till 3:00AM again." The Bible uses the term *lest* in a similar way.

When Pharaoh let the people go, God did not lead them by way of the land of the Philistines, although that was near. For God said, "*Lest* the people change their minds when they see war and return to Egypt" (Ex. 13:17). Another example was Cain, where the Lord put a mark on him, "*lest* any who found him should attack him" (Gen. 4:15). And then there was Gideon, who was told by God to reduce the size of his army, "*lest* Israel boast over me, saying, 'my own hand has saved me'" (Judg. 7:2).

Human beings have, at times, said or done things that interfered with God's big-picture plans for the world, and in those cases, God would temporarily suspend their self-governing ability. He did this with a witchdoctor named Balaam who was hired by the king of Moab to put a curse on Israel. When he opened his mouth to pronounce the curse, however, God changed it into a blessing (Neh. 13:2). Balaam had no choice in the matter.

And then there's Pharaoh, whose heart God hardened to fulfill his sovereign purpose for the nation of Israel. God was not going to allow this human being to get in the way of the promises he had made to Abram (Gen. 15:18), even if it meant having to override his free will. Everything God does on a strategic level will *always* come to pass, whether people choose to cooperate with him or not. He says, "My counsel shall stand, and I will accomplish all my purpose" (Isa. 46:10). It should be noted, however, that whenever God overrides a person's free will, two things are always in play:

- The first is that the disengagement of their self-governing abilities is always temporary. As soon as God has finished using them for his sovereign purposes, their free will is reinstated. He overruled the plans of Pharaoh and Balaam, but only until *his* plans had come to pass.

- Secondly, the removal of the person's free will never has anything to do with their individual relationship with God. In both of these cases, the individuals God used had already made up their mind to oppose him. Let's not forget that Pharaoh hardened his own heart five times before God decided to harden it further. Whenever a person hardens their heart toward God, they become a candidate for him to use them without their permission!

Other examples exist, but what is important to understand is that this is *not* the way God works most of the time. Instead, he looks for those who will align themselves with his will. If they are headed in the wrong direction, he tries to woo them back to himself. He might even orchestrate the circumstances surrounding them to make it easier for them to go his way.

My life is an example of this. When I was a teenager, I was running from God. On Christmas morning 1976, I lay awake in a jail cell in Amsterdam, The Netherlands, thinking of my family back in Australia. My journey had taken me to Panama,

Ecuador, Peru, Bolivia and Argentina. Then, it was off to Europe to trek the famed *Hippie Trail* that went from The Netherlands to India and Nepal. But God had other plans. I was arrested, thrown in jail, and three days later put on a KLM flight back to Sydney. I wasn't happy, especially that I would not be able to meet up with friends who were waiting for me in Athens. But I am so grateful now.

A few months after returning home, I remembered that God warned me this was going to happen. The night before I left Sydney, I was pulled into a prayer meeting in our family's living room where one of my mother's friends laid her hands on me and prophesied: "God wants to say to you, young man, that his hand will be upon you as you go … but you won't like it." And that is exactly what happened.

It was perhaps the clearest example to me of how God deals with his wayward children. He doesn't *force* them to come back to him. Instead, he orchestrates circumstances surrounding their lives to make it *easier* for them to come back to him. Like the Lost Son in Jesus' story. His life had become so miserable in that foreign land the only thing he could think about was returning home to his loving father. This is the crucial distinction we have to make: Influence is different than force. Once I was back in Australia, my life took a 180-degree turn in the direction of God. I went to a one-week outreach with YWAM in Canberra, rededicated my life to Christ, and never looked back again.

What is it precisely that God does to draw people back to him? It is "a persuasion" rather than "a coercion," Greg Boyd explains.[15] He woos the prodigals to come home, but even when he does this, it is still possible for them to resist him.

This brings to the forefront, even more sharply than before, a key theological detail: The Apostle Paul tells us God, "works all things according to the counsel of his will" (Eph. 1:11), which is often understood to mean that God *causes* everything to happen according to the counsel of his will. A better interpretation of this passage, however, is to say God *steers* circumstances *in the direction* of his will, because the root word translated "works" in this passage is *energeō*, from which comes our English word "energize." *Energeō* means: To be operative, to be at work, to put forth power, or to aid someone. In other words, God moves people in the direction of his will, but like Roger Forster points out, "it's not an irresistible directive power, but rather, a stimulation."[16]

All this to say, God allows man to retain his free will in spite of suffering, because free will is more important than the absence of suffering. "Without free will," Dean Sherman explains, "we would be less than human."[17]

WHEN IT WOULD BE MORALLY WRONG

The second reason God does not intervene when things go wrong, is when it would be morally wrong for him to do so. Many sermons have been preached on man's responsibility to do what is right, but what is not as commonly addressed is God's commitment to do the same. He didn't only invent morality for humans. He invented it for himself as well! When he says, "You must be holy," it is because he is holy (1 Pet. 1:16). When he tells us to "forgive," (Col. 3:13) it is because that is what he does (Luke 23:34). When he says, "Love your neighbor," it is because he first loved us (1 John 4:19). The ultimate example of God's subjection to his own moral law took place at Calvary, when he accepted his own unbreakable terms of justice.

It might seem absurd that the sovereign ruler of the universe would choose to subject himself to the same laws prescribed to his finite creation, especially when you consider that he doesn't *have to* do this. No one is going to hold his feet to the fire if he decides to give himself a pass. He is the highest authority. Who is going to tell him what he can or cannot do? But his decision to abide by his own laws is the ultimate example of someone who lives what he preaches. How I love that about him!

As we advance steadily toward the heart of the matter, it will serve us well to make a distinction between *physical* and *moral* law. It is this distinction that best clarifies the reason God will sometimes refrain from getting involved in the affairs of man. Author Winkie Pratney puts it this way: "Physical law is the way something *always* behaves. Someone slipping off a fourteen-story building has no choice but to fall, and 8 X 8 cannot optionally be 15. Physical law leaves no choice. It describes rules of action, what is true in the interlocking relationships of space, time and matter. Find what is true, define it, and you will have physical law," he says. In God's universe, things maintain the fixed relationships to each other that we discover in the sciences. "But God, though he runs creation by physical laws, gave moral beings a different and higher order of law: *moral law.* Moral law does not describe the way moral beings *do* behave; it describes the way moral beings *ought to* behave."[18]

Charles Finney defined moral law as, "the rule for the government of free and intelligent action as opposed to necessity and unintelligent action. It is the law of liberty, as opposed to the law of necessity—of motive and free choice as opposed to force."[19] In other words, if there is no choice involved, no intelligent action allowed, no possible option, then the rule is physical, not moral.

This raises a key question, the answer to which will shape the way we see God in the light of suffering. "We know that we are moral beings, but is God a moral being also?" asks Pratney. "Not only in the sense of being able to differentiate between good and evil, but in the sense of having his own infinite freedom to choose."[20]

In humans, the intentions of the will resolve into choices. When someone wills an end, they know they *could* will differently. A person is genuinely free to make any end his goal, but is it also this way with God? Is he free to choose however he pleases? And the answer must be, can *only* be, yes. This fact is made abundantly clear in that, human beings, God's primary image-bearers in the world, have been endowed with this same faculty (Gen. 1:26). Like us, God can do whatever he pleases, and with absolute impunity, but he never does because, as one great man of God put it, "He considers the principles of moral law to be as binding upon himself as they are upon his moral creatures."[21] This decision by God, however, puts him in a difficult position.

Billy Graham described God's predicament as *a divine dilemma*. Because he loves man, he does not want to cast him aside, but because he is holy, he cannot ignore his rebellion altogether.[22] He has to take everything into account, always evaluating man's actions in the light of what man knows he *should have* done. What complicates matters further is that this responsibility is different for every person. It all depends on their understanding of what is right and wrong. The greater their knowledge, the greater their responsibility to live up to that knowledge (Luke 12:48). As we glimpsed in Chapter 9, God would never hold a child to the same moral standards as a mature adult. The same is true of someone who is mentally handicapped, whose capacity to discern right from wrong is greatly reduced.

God takes everything into account, and then decides if he can intervene on our behalf when we ask him. Unfortunately, if his intervention violates the principles of morality, he won't do it. He is a God who, "does no wrong" (Deut. 32:4 NLT). Never. Although he desires to reach out in love and mercy to every person in every situation, his commitment to moral integrity requires that he do this *only to the extent* that his holiness and justice are not compromised.

All this, I suggest, has been made perfectly clear in the scriptures. We are told God is the Almighty (Rev. 19:6), that he upholds all things by the word of his power (Heb. 1:3), and that *nothing* is too difficult for him (Luke 1:37). In other words, God can do anything he wants! But then it says in another place that God cannot (or will not) tell a lie (Titus 1:2). Is this a contradiction in the Bible? No. These passages only make sense if we separate what is *physical* from what is *moral*. Obviously God has the physical ability to say something that is untrue, but he never will, because that would be morally wrong. He lives within the same moral parameters he gave to us. Astonishing but true!

FOR JUSTICE TO PREVAIL, THE LAW MUST BE KING

When there is justice in a society, it is only because the people respect the rule of law. In the seventeenth century, Scottish pastor, Samuel Rutherford, explained this brilliantly in his book, *Lex, Rex* which in Latin means, the law is king. It was intended to be a defense of the Scottish Presbyterian ideal in politics in which Rutherford advocated for limited government and constitutionalism in politics.

Constitutionalism is a system that requires everybody, including government officials, to be subject to the limitations of a higher law. In other words, the law must be king, not the other way around. It establishes *the rule of law* as the ultimate standard within a society, as opposed to the arbitrary judgments or self-serving edicts of public officials. Constitutionalism states that government officials are not free to do whatever they please because they are bound to observe both the limitations on power and the procedures that have been set out in the constitutional law of the community in which they serve. Constitutionalism is basically the concept of limited government under a higher law. This, argues author Vishal Mangalwadi, is what led America's founders to reject Greek democracy in favor of a constitutional republic, because it required that the power of the people *and* the decisions made by their leaders, be constrained by the rule of law.[23]

In *Lex, Rex,* Rutherford used arguments from Scripture, natural law, and Scottish law, along with a Huguenot tract entitled *Vindiciae Contra Tyrannos,* to attack royal absolutism and argue in favor of the rule of law. He stated that in any just society *the law* must be king (Lex Rex), but if the order is reversed (Rex Lex), it would lead to injustice within that society. Political and religious leaders of the day accused Rutherford of high treason, but he was never prosecuted because he died before the charge could be tried. *Lex Rex* itself was burned in Edinburgh and St. Andrews, where Rutherford had been the principal of the university. But the ideas he espoused became foundational for future governments, because the principles are timeless, and as useful today as they were in the seventeenth century.

The reason nations like Switzerland and Japan, have strong economies is not primarily because of their higher education, advances in technology or personal integrity. The big difference-maker is *the rule of law.*[24] If someone commits a crime in Switzerland or Japan, be they the CEO of a multinational corporation, a well-loved and respected public figure, or even the political head of the country, in almost every case, they will be held accountable for their actions. This, then, forces everyone else to rise to a higher moral standard as well. The result is prosperity, peace, and stability in the society at large. As John Rawls once put it: When a society is regulated by a public sense of justice, it is inherently stable.

An example of Lex Rex took place in the United States in 1974 when President Richard Nixon resigned rather than face removal from office for his role in one of the biggest scandals in U.S. history. So he stepped down. Contrast this with some nations where the leader and his family live opulent and corrupt lifestyles. They are rarely held accountable for their abuse of power and contempt for the rule of law, and the result is their people suffer.

This brings to the forefront a pivotal question: When it comes to God, is it Rex Lex or Lex Rex? "Does he just make up what is right and wrong?" asks Winkie Pratney. "Does he play by the same rules as us, or is it rather, that because he gets to make up the rules, whatever he says goes?"[25] Is he above the law, or does he live within the parameters of the law? And, as unbelievable as it might seem, the God of the Bible lives according to *the same rules* he gave to man. It is the primary reason Jesus had to come and die for our sins. It was the only way for God to marry justice and mercy.

This concept is explained brilliantly in the story of a king and the people he loved. Over the course of time the king noticed that violence was increasing within his kingdom. So he ordered an investigation, and it was discovered that immorality was rampant throughout the land. His response was swift but severe. Anyone caught in any immoral behavior would have their eyes gouged out. People immediately changed their behavior and soon violence began to decrease. It was the exact outcome the king was hoping for.

One day, however, the king's only son was caught in an adulterous affair with a married woman and brought before him in the central city square. His subjects gathered around to see what the king would do. He had to decide. Who did he love more, his son or his law? If he disregarded his law, he would lose the respect of his people and his law would be of no effect. On the other hand, he loved his son, and couldn't bear to see him living out the rest of his days in darkness.

Finally, he was ready to pronounce his verdict. He ordered his guards to gouge out his son's right eye, but what he did next no one expected. He commanded that they untie his son and let him go free. He then took his place, ordering his men to gouge out his own left eye, and by doing so, he upheld his law, but showed mercy to his son. And that is what God did. In his infinite love and wisdom, he found a way to forgive us and still be just!

For many years what troubled me most in the Bible was the death of Job's ten children. Job's boils and the destruction of his property could be explained as a test, but how could God allow his innocent children to die? It seemed like they were nothing more than collateral damage in God's determination to win his wager with Satan (Job 1:8-12). But upon closer evaluation something stands out in the text that might explain why God did not prevent Satan from attacking them.

The Bible says God is a shield to those who walk in integrity (Prov. 2:7) and he protects those who fear him (Ps. 34:7). But what if a person is living outside the boundaries of God's protective shield? What if they are living in sin and have no fear of God? Would that change things? Would God still be able to shield them from the powers of darkness if and when they were targeted? Clearly God has the physical power to stop Satan, but in the moral sense would he intervene if Satan had a *legal right* to attack them?

In his seven fantasy novels, *The Chronicles of Narnia*, C.S Lewis addresses this very subject. My mother used to read the books to my sisters and me at bedtime when we were young. I must have heard the entire series five or six times. One of the principles that made an impact on my life comes from the second novel, *The Lion, the Witch and the Wardrobe*. In one scene, the white witch, an evil queen representing Satan, is contending with Aslan for the life of Edmund. He was one of the four young protagonists of the story, and Aslan, a lion, who represented Jesus. In Edmund's greed and lust for power, he had sold his soul to the witch, but when he realized the error of his ways, it was too late. Now, captive, and with no visible way of escape, his only hope was for someone to come in from the outside and rescue him.

In order to liberate Edmund from the white witch's evil grasp, someone would have to die in his place, a principle she made abundantly clear. "The Magic which the Emperor put into Narnia at the very beginning," she boasted, "was that every traitor belongs to me as my lawful prey and that for every treachery I have a right to a kill."[26] As you are reading, it suddenly dawns on you. She is telling the truth, which is brought forth in the final scene when Aslan gives his own life in exchange for the boy.

Within the story of Job, we see the same principle brought forth. Job's children might not have been as innocent as I originally thought. They would regularly hold feasts in their homes (Job 1:4). Harmless enough it would seem, except for one important detail that is often overlooked: Alcohol was involved (Job 1:13). How much alcohol is unclear, but a clue might lie in the fact that Job would offer a sacrifice on behalf of his children at the conclusion of each party (Job 1:5). The Bible does not explicitly say they were engaging in sinful activities at these parties, but there is enough in the text to suggest this might have been the case. If this were so, then, it would explain why Satan had a legal right to attack them, and why God might have chosen not to intervene.

PERSONAL APPLICATION

How has unanswered prayer affected your relationship with God?

Most of us pray when things go wrong, but God does not always answer prayer the way we want him to. In some instances it almost seems he is ignoring us altogether, and this can have a negative effect on our relationship with him. If you're struggling because God is distant, or silent, or you feel he hasn't intervened when you needed, fortunately, there is something you can do about it. I call it the pathway to freedom, and it's really not that complicated. The only ingredients necessary for the journey are pencil, paper, time and complete honesty.

Step #1: Go back in your mind to the place and time you felt rejected by God. What happened? Recalling it might be painful, but bringing it to the surface is the first step toward the breakthrough.

Step #2: Identify the feeling by name: How did it make you feel when this happened? Did you feel abandoned, guilty, defeated, afraid?

Step #3: Ask God where he was when this took place. Why weren't you there? Why didn't you intervene? He won't be offended by your honesty.

Step #4: It's okay to get angry. People sometimes bury their feelings, especially when it relates to God, because they assume it would be disrespectful to tell him how they really feel. But this is a mistake. God knows our feelings are real, although not necessarily accurate, and facing them head-on is absolutely essential.

In 1969, psychiatrist Elisabeth Kübler-Ross introduced the "Five Stages of Grief," based on her studies of patients facing terminal illness. It was later discovered, however, that people often experience the same feelings during other types of negative life challenges too. These are the five stages she identified:

1. Denial: "This can't be happening to me."
2. Anger: "*Why* is this happening? Whose fault is it?"

3. Bargaining: "If you make this go away, I will do this for you in return."
4. Depression: "I'm so sad I can't go on."
5. Acceptance (or resolution): "I'm finally at peace with what happened."

The problem is, if we skip over anger, we run the risk of getting stuck in an endless cycle of depression, never arriving at a place of resolution because the anger is still pent up deep inside of us. So get angry about what happened to you. Tell God how you *really* feel.

Step #5: Let God speak to you: Giving him an opportunity to tell you what happened from his perspective is a crucial step in your healing process. What is he saying? It might be, "I wasn't the one who did this," or "It broke my heart too," or "It was that person's selfishness that caused this to happen." God speaks the truth, and the truth is the only thing that ultimately sets people free (John 8:32).

Step #6: If God doesn't speak to you immediately, choose to trust him. I have experienced times when God doesn't speak to me for days, or weeks, or even months. "Every day I call to you but you don't answer," David complained (Ps. 22:2). He, too, felt God was ignoring him, yet he never stopped trusting God. And this is important: Feelings of abandonment are not necessarily an indication God doesn't care, because Jesus experienced these same feelings on the cross (Matt. 27:46). So tell God you trust him. Don't block him out. He wants to walk this pathway toward freedom alongside of you.

CHAPTER ELEVEN

Those who lay down their lives

He is no fool who gives what he cannot keep,
to gain what he cannot lose.

—JIM ELLIOT

In his critically acclaimed book, *End of the Spear,* Steve Saint recounts the story of his dad, Nate, and four of his missionary colleagues, who were killed by a primitive tribe in South America. It is a continuation of Elisabeth Elliot's bestseller, *Through Gates of Splendor.* Both describe Operation Auca, in which these dedicated young men attempted to evangelize the Huaorani people of the tropical rain forest of eastern Ecuador.

On January 8, 1956, Jim Elliot, Nate Saint, Ed McCully, Roger Youderian and Pete Flemming set up camp on a sandbar along the Curaray River, a few kilometers downstream from the Huaorani settlement. Although rumored to be violent savages, God had given these five men a deep love for this Stone-Age people group. They hoped to introduce them to Jesus.

After months of prayer and preparation, they eagerly awaited a face-to-face encounter with the Huaorani. Tragically, their efforts came to an abrupt end when warriors attacked their camp and speared them to death. Why didn't God warn them of what was about to take place? He knew the Huaorani were afraid of the cowodi (outsiders) and that they would defend their territory.

As they dragged their bodies into the river, they talked among themselves. "The cowodi had guns in their plane. Why hadn't they used them to defend themselves?"[1] The reason was the missionaries had decided long before they would be willing to lay down their lives if it came to that. They were there to share the love of Christ. How could they retaliate, even if it was in self-defense?

"They came to tell you God has a son," explained Dayuma, the first Huaorani to come to Christ. It took time, but eventually the rest of them understood too. "He was also speared but didn't spear back," she explained, "so the people spearing him could one day live well."

NO ONE TOOK HIS LIFE

Two years later, the wife of one of the missionaries, and the sister of another, moved to the jungle to live with the people who had killed the men they loved. They wanted to complete their unfinished mission. Nine year-old Steve Saint went with them, choosing to stay, and live with one of the Huaorani families who took him in as their own. It wasn't until years later he came to discover that Mincaye, the man of the family, was one of those who had speared his dad.

What was Steve supposed to do? Avenge his father's death? That was what the Huaorani expected. Or maybe he should leave Ecuador altogether. But Mincaye was now a different man from the violent warrior who had once lived by the creed, "kill or be killed." He had become a Christian, and his life had been transformed. And there was another complicating factor.

Steve had come to love Mincaye. "I have never gotten over the heartache of losing my dad," he said, "but I can't imagine my life without Mincaye either."

Many people struggle to understand this. One of them, a USA Today reporter, commented after hearing Steve's testimony that if he were in his shoes, he could "Forgive Mincaye, maybe ... but love him? that is morbid." But it was not morbid to Steve. "In the natural my relationship with Mincaye doesn't make any sense," he said, "unless, you put God into the equation." Yes, his dad's death was painful, but Mincaye would never have come to Christ if his dad had never gone to Ecuador. Neither would dozens of other Huaorani who became believers too. Add to this the tens of thousands of others whose lives were impacted when they heard what happened. Many of them volunteered to go to other unreached people groups. The ultimate reality of what happened sank in as Steve pondered what had taken place. "No one took my father's life," he said. "He gave it."

GOD LOOKS FOR VOLUNTEERS

God never forces anyone to serve him, especially if the road ahead involves sacrifice. He searches for those who will volunteer. He waits for someone, anyone really, who will say, "Here am I, send me." The prophet Isaiah was one such person. God allowed him to overhear a private conversation between the Father, Son, and Holy Spirit where they were discussing who they could send to deliver a hard word to the people. "Who will go for us?" he heard them say.

God could have sent an angel to deliver the difficult message, but he didn't. Instead, he allowed Isaiah to know his heart so he would have an opportunity to volunteer. "Here am I!" Isaiah said, "send me" (Isa. 6:8). Those were the exact words God was hoping to hear.

Isaiah wasn't killed for speaking the Word of the Lord like some of those who went before him, but let the record show that going in Jesus' name often meant persecution of some kind, and even death (Luke 13:34). Only a century ago, missionaries would purchase one-way tickets to their final destination. And instead of suitcases, they would pack their belongings into a coffin. They understood that when they returned home, it would probably be inside that wooden box.

A.W. Milne was one such missionary. He felt God calling him to Vanuatu in the South Pacific. All his predecessors had been killed by the local headhunters but that didn't matter to Milne. Like Isaiah, he told the Lord he would go. He was ready to lay down his life if necessary, but surprisingly, they never killed him. For 35 years, he lived among the people of Vanuatu and led many of them to Christ. When he finally died, the tribe buried him in the village, a great honor for a foreigner, and on his tombstone they inscribed: "When he came, there was no light. When he left, there was no darkness"[2]

THE GREATEST EXAMPLE

The greatest example of someone who laid down his life for others is Jesus himself. He didn't have to come to earth. He wanted to come to earth. His willingness to leave the beauty and majesty of heaven was born out of an impassioned love for his fallen creation. It's like Ben Fielding and Brooke Ligertwood put in one of their songs: "you didn't want heaven without us," they wrote.[3] He had created man to spend eternity alongside of him, and he knew it wouldn't be the same without us.

Caiaphas, Pilate, and all the others thought they had won a great victory the day they crucified Jesus, but what they didn't understand was that this was all part of the plan. They didn't take his life. He laid it down of his own accord (John 10:18). At any moment, he could have summoned legions of angels to come to his defense (Matt. 26:53). The truth is, he could have broken their measly restraints all by himself if he had wanted to. He was God. Nothing is too hard for him. But he didn't. He stuck to the plan—the one he and the Father had conceived long before the world began (Rev. 13:8). He had tried to tell his disciples about it on several occasions, but they never seemed to be listening. Later, it all made sense.

THE WAY THE VICTORY IS WON

One of the dangers of our familiarity with the story of Christ's crucifixion is that we could convince ourselves it was a one-off event, and that from now on, no one else would have to suffer. The opposite is actually the case, N.T. Wright points out: "Yes, the victory was indeed won, launched through the suffering of Jesus. But it is now implemented, and put into effective operation, by the suffering of his people."[4]

This is why Paul could write unapologetically that the servants of God are commended, "By their afflictions, hardships, calamities, beatings, imprisonments, riots, labors, sleepless nights, and hunger (2 Cor. 6:4-5). He went on: "We are treated as impostors," he said, "and yet are true; as unknown, and yet well known; as dying, and behold, we live; as punished, and yet not killed; as sorrowful, yet always rejoicing; as poor, yet making many rich; as having nothing, yet possessing everything" (2 Cor. 6: 8-10).

It was hard for Paul's audience to understand this. They lived, as we do, in a society where everyone was eager to look good, to be successful, and to impress their neighbors. The beaten, bedraggled figure of Paul was hardly that of a leader one might be proud of. Yet Paul demonstrates that this is the Messiah's pattern. This is how the victory is won!

African bishop Tertullian, writing around AD 200, reflected this same perspective when he said, "the blood of the martyrs is the seed of the church." It is not a picture that is easily captured, let alone embraced by the comfortable Western church, yet it is, without question, the way we are called to follow Jesus. Taking up our cross is what makes us one of his disciples (Luke 14:27).

THE ISSUE THAT ALWAYS SEEMS TO COME UP

The issue that always seems to come up when there is unnecessary suffering is God's justice. If you love him, you want to defend him, but sometimes there are no good answers, at least none that will fully satisfy everyone. If God is all-powerful, people reason, doesn't his non-involvement make him at least partially responsible for the bad things that happen in the world? Some even speculate that God is involved in every single event that takes place. But is that true?

"Does God reach down and slightly twist the wheels of a school bus, and then watch it career through a guardrail?" Philip Yancey asks. "Does he draw a red pencil line through a map of Indiana to plot the exact path of a tornado? There, hit that house, kill that six-year-old, but skip over this next house. Does he program the earth like a video game, constantly experimenting with tidal waves, seismic temblors, and hurricanes?"[5] Those who have been given pat answers to their questions about God's justice are prone to blame him for the evil and suffering they see in the world, or if nothing else, to distance themselves from him. Others have dealt with their pain by questioning if a just and loving God exists at all.

Our innate sense of fairness demands an explanation for the injustices we see in our world. Why do bad things happen to good people? If God were truly just, bad things would only happen to bad people! "Why didn't God prevent this from happening to us?" asked Keeley Lange, one of our young staff moms. Her question echoed the sentiment of many of the other staff and students too. Even some of those who seemed the strongest in their faith were rattled by the events that had just taken place.

THE MOMENT THE PENNY DROPPED

I want to take you back to the day before the shootings, because something happened that completely changed my mind about what took place. My wife and I had just returned from out of town and I headed over to the YWAM base for our Friday morning worship. Matthew Murray was at his house a few miles down the road, plotting the events that would change our lives forever.

The theme of our morning worship was revival. Someone spoke of the need for spiritual awakening in this generation. They described how most revivals in history began during a time of crisis that turned people's focus back to God. Stacey Miller, one of our leaders, called for a personal response. "If you want to ask God to use your life to make a powerful impact on your generation, regardless of the cost, would you come forward, and we will pray for you?" In a room of roughly two hundred people, twenty moved quietly to the middle of the room. And that was it. We prayed for them and went on with the rest of our day. The next evening the shootings took place.

A week later, one of our other leaders, John Murphy, told me something that made me rethink everything that had happened. "Philip and Tiffany went forward last week," he said. I didn't get what he was trying to say at first, but then he added, "although Dan and Charlie remained seated. They didn't go forward like the other two." And that's when the penny dropped.

Dan and Charlie survived the shooting, even though Dan was hit in the neck, the bullet miraculously missing his windpipe, jugular vein, and spinal cord. Was it just a fluke, or did God somehow have a hand in the outcome? Is it just possible, I thought to myself, that God allowed Philip and Tiffany to be taken because they asked him to use them to make an impact on their generation? Everything within me wanted to reject the notion that God would allow something like this to happen simply because two people went forward in a worship service. And how was he going to use them now that they were gone? The answer will stop you dead in your tracks, but first there is something else we need to address.

LIVING FOR A HEAVENLY REWARD

Even a casual reading of the New Testament reveals that our lives *do not* end with death. God has been preparing an eternal dwelling place for those who love him. "In my Father's house are many rooms," Jesus said. "If it were not so, I would have told you" (John 14:2). The beauty and majesty of that place promises to exceed even our wildest dreams. "No eye has seen, nor ear heard, nor the heart of man imagined, what God has prepared for those who love him" (1 Cor. 2:9).

And all the saints of history will be there too. It will be the occasion of God's final reckoning with man. Nothing will be held back. Those who were never recognized on earth will be brought forward, including those who lost their lives for the cause of Christ. He has been keeping a tally of everything. "And my reward is with me," he says, "to give to each person according to what they have done" (Rev. 22:12 NIV). There are four groups who will receive their reward on that day.

- The first to come forward will be those who helped the poor, and needy, without receiving compensation. "When you give a dinner or a banquet," Jesus said, "do not invite your friends or your brothers or your relatives or rich neighbors, lest they also invite you in return and you be repaid. But when you give a feast, invite the poor, the crippled, the lame, the blind, and you will be blessed, because they cannot repay you. For you will be repaid at the resurrection of the just" (Luke 14:12-14).

- The second group will be those who took care of God's people. This includes pastors and priests, Sunday school teachers, coaches, mentors, and anyone, basically, who has dedicated their life to shepherd the flock of God. "And when the chief Shepherd appears," Peter said, "you will receive the unfading crown of glory" (1 Pet. 5:2-4).

- The third contingent will be those who were persecuted for their faith in Christ. "Blessed are you when people hate you and when they exclude you and revile you and spurn your name as evil, on account of the Son of Man!" Jesus said. "Rejoice in that day, and leap for joy, for behold, your reward is great in heaven ..." (Luke 6:22-23).

- The final group will be those who lost their lives while serving Jesus. "Whoever loses his life for my sake will find it," Jesus promised (Matt. 16:25). He then described the day of his final return, when he will personally repay each person, "according to what he has done" (Matt. 16: 27).

But aren't people a little naïve, someone asked, for living their lives for a future heavenly reward? C.T Studd didn't think so. He gave away his entire fortune, including his inheritance and a promising athletic career to go as a missionary to the Belgian Congo. "If Jesus Christ be God and died for me," he said on one occasion, "then there is no sacrifice too great for me to make for him."

So too, Dietrich Bonhoeffer, who was one of the most brilliant minds of his generation. When World War II broke out in Europe, he found himself in the comparative safety of the United States, and yet he knew God was calling him to return to his native Germany. He joined the campaign against Hitler, knowing well where it might lead. His Letters and Papers from

Prison, tell its own story of profound reflection and prayer as he faced the hangman's noose. Who can say what wonderful works he might have authored had he survived? But who can tell what impact his faithful life and witness have had precisely through his martyrdom?"[6]

And, of course, who can forget Jim Elliot, who did not consider it a waste to lay down his life for Christ. "He is no fool," he said, "who gives what he cannot keep, to gain what he cannot lose." Was it foolish of him to think this way? Not according to Jesus. "Do not lay up for yourselves treasures on earth," he exhorted his disciples, "lay up for yourselves treasures in heaven" (Matt. 6:19-20).

Like these fallen heroes of the faith, I believe Philip and Tiffany lost their lives for the cause of Christ. They asked him to use them and he did. I can picture Jesus saying to them one day, "Thank you for being willing to give your lives that others might come to know me. You were grains of wheat that fell to the ground and died, but your sacrifice has produced much fruit (John 12:24). See these thousands standing before me? You never met them personally, but they came to know me because of your story." I can't wait to witness this firsthand. I will be one of those standing to my feet and cheering at the top of my lungs. Who, you ask, are these thousands standing before Jesus? Let me tell you the rest of the story.

JESUS FREAKS

Only one life, 'twill soon be past,
Only what's done for Christ will last.
And when I am dying, how happy I'll be,
If the lamp of my life has been burned out for Thee—C.T. Studd

Everything began with a married couple, Charles and Katherine Cobb, who owned a production company. DTS had such a profound impact on them they wanted to show others what happens when young people surrender their lives to God. Their plan was to produce a movie of our Snowboarders DTS, and then, use it as a pilot for a reality TV show. Students were told ahead of time there would be cameras everywhere. They came anyway—45 of them.

We called the movie Jesus Freaks, because of how perfectly it describes this radical subculture when they get fired up for God. But one person was missing—Tiffany. She was supposed to be on the staff of that DTS. The Production Company decided to use the actual 9-1-1 recording from the shootings as the first scene of the movie. It was powerful. You can hear Charlie in the background calling the operator. "I've been shot in the legs," he says, "and my friend was shot in the neck." And then a few moments later, "Are people coming yet?"

"Yes, honey," the operator says, "they're almost there."

Throughout the entire movie, Philip and Tiffany are constantly remembered, their story playing a central role in the entire production.

In the years that followed, teams from our YWAM base fanned out across the globe to show Jesus Freaks. I showed it personally to audiences in Europe, Australia and North America. Everywhere I went young people would rush to the front and dedicate their lives to Christ—some of them for the very first time. And on each occasion I kept thinking: Philip and Tiffany are watching all of this from heaven.

Is it possible God allowed Matthew Murray's evil, hateful act to bring about the opposite of what he intended ... the saving of many lives? Consider this: When Tiffany's friends went through her belongings the week after the shootings they found her journal. In it were two scriptures, her last entries, and one of them was Genesis 50:20: "You intended to harm me, but God intended it for good to accomplish what is now being done, the saving of many lives."

PERSONAL APPLICATION

What steps are you taking to follow in Jesus' footsteps?

There is, at the heart of the New Testament, a clear and uncompromising message: You cannot be a disciple of Jesus unless you take up your cross and follow him (Luke 14:27). Our usual understanding of Jesus' mandate is one of self-denial. Of our need to cut back on the excesses and pleasures of this earthly life. But clearly, Jesus is asking for much more than that.

Even if we are willing to give up *most* of the things we love and hold dear, it is still not enough for him. This was what the rich young ruler found out. He was willing to do everything Jesus asked except one thing: give up his riches (Luke 18:22). The point we cannot afford to miss is that this was not about money. Jesus only brought up the man's wealth because that was the one thing holding him back.

Believers in the first century would have had no trouble understanding this was what it meant to follow Jesus, and many of them did, indeed, pay the ultimate price. For most of us it will probably never come to that, but we must still be willing to give him everything. Unfortunately, many have come to Christ on a false premise. "You will be fulfilled if you come to Jesus," we are told. "He wants to bless you and make you happy." But these promised blessings appeal mostly to our ego and self-interest. The idea that we should lay down our lives is a radical departure from what many of us have been taught, but it is the essence of the gospel message. Once we make that decision, every other decision is easy.

Fifty years ago, a group of believers gathered in a small cottage in a remote region of the former Soviet Union. They had come to worship, fellowship, and hear the word of God. Suddenly, the front door swung open and in came two men in long overcoats holding automatic weapons. "If any of you are not true Christians you must leave immediately," one of them demanded. At that, several people got up hastily and left. Only six or seven remained. When the door closed, the men put down their guns. "We are also Christians," they said, "and we have an important message to share with you. We just wanted to make sure there were no spies in your midst."

So what about you? Are you willing to take up your cross and follow Jesus? It is not a decision any of us should make lightly, nor impulsively, because it could be the most sacrificial decision we ever make. It certainly was for Philip and Tiffany. It might not cost you your life as it did for them, but it might cost you a promising career, or a job promotion, or the opportunity to make a significant amount of money. It might deprive you of the chance to get married and have children one day. God might tell you leave your home, and everything you hold dear, to serve him as a missionary in a distant land.

This was the case with Margaret Clarkson, who accepted the job nobody else wanted, that of a schoolteacher in a remote gold mining town in northern Ontario. It was a lonely place for a single woman in the 1940s, but she knew she was exactly where God wanted her. The poem she wrote, born out of a life fully surrendered to Christ, became perhaps the greatest missionary hymn of the 20th century:

So send I you to labour unrewarded
To serve unpaid, unloved, unsought, unknown
To bear rebuke, to suffer scorn and scoffing
So send I you to toil for Me alone

So send I you to bind the bruised and broken
Over wandering souls to work, to weep, to wake
To bear the burdens of a world that's weary
So send I you to suffer for My sake

So send I you to loneliness and longing
With a heart made hungry for the loved and known
Forsaking kin and kindred, friend and dear one
So send I you to know My love alone

So send I you to leave your life's ambition
To die to dear desire, self-will resign
To labor long, and love where men revile you
So send I you to lose your life in Mine

So send I you to hearts made hard by hatred
To eyes made blind because they will not see
To spend, though it be blood, to spend and spare not
So send I you to taste of Calvary

And in one final climactic declaration, the song concludes with Christ's last commission to the church: "As the Father has sent me, so send I you"[7]

CONCLUSION

I began this project on a journey to discover the truth about God and the issue of suffering, even if that truth turned out to be painful. The burden of proof, I felt, rested with God, not man, because he is the one who said in his Word that he is just (Rom. 9:14), and loving (1 John 4:8), and faithful in everything he does (Ps. 145:17). I also wanted to hear the backstory, from his point of view, of why four innocent people lost their lives at the hands of a shooter in 2007.

After completing thousands of hours of research, prayer, and conversations on the topic, my verdict is that the accusations against God are unfounded. From what I have seen, most of these claims are based on a false premise: That if God is all-powerful, he is ultimately responsible for the bad things that happen in his world. My conclusion is different. In 6,000 years of human history, I would argue there are only a few instances in which God is the author of suffering, and in those instances, his actions are morally justified.

He is not the bloodthirsty tyrant some have made him out to be. Neither is he a disinterested bystander who could care less what happens to man. The scriptures paint a far different picture of who he is. He, too, is brokenhearted over the way things have turned out. I admit that mysteries remain. Like the apostle Paul, I accept that some things are impossible to comprehend (Rom. 11:33), and for those I choose to trust God. But aside from a handful of these mysteries, I have satisfied my own need for understanding.

I have become convinced of this one thing, that although we live in a broken world filled with broken people, God has done his part to remedy the situation. He gave his life to mend our damaged relationship with him, and he is more than willing to walk alongside us as an ever-present help in times of trouble. What is more, he has promised a redo of everything that was lost in The Fall. The "old order" of things will soon pass away, and God will make all things new again.

YOU'RE NOT HOME YET!

*A*n *elderly missionary couple was returning to the U.S. after forty years in Africa. Their plan was to retire in New York City. As their ship steamed into New York Harbor, they reflected on their bleak situation. They had no pension, their health was failing, and they were fearful of what the future might hold. They couldn't help comparing themselves to one of the other passengers who had boarded the same ship on the other side of the Atlantic— the recently retired President of the United States, Teddy Roosevelt, who was returning from a big-game hunting safari in British East Africa.*

As the ship pulled past the Statue of Liberty and into the harbor, they could hear a band playing on the dock. A huge crowd had gathered to welcome the returning president. The old missionary turned and said to his wife, "We have given our lives in faithful service for God all these years, and this man comes back from hunting animals and everybody makes a big fuss over him, but nobody gives two hoots about us."

"Dear," his wife replied, "you shouldn't feel that way. Try not to be bitter about it."

"I just can't help it," he replied. "It's not right. After all, if God is running this world, why does he permit such an injustice?" As the boat neared the dock, and the sound of the band and the cheering grew louder, the missionary became more and more depressed. The mayor of New York City was on hand to greet the returning president, along with many other dignitaries—but no one even noticed the missionary and his wife. They slipped off the ship and

found a cheap flat on the east side, hoping the next day to see what they could do to make a living in the city.

That night the man's spirit broke. "I can't take this anymore!" he said to his wife, "God is not fair! We don't even know anyone who can help us, or where we should go. If God is truly faithful, why hasn't he met our needs? Well, why don't you ask Him?" said his wife. "All right," said the man. "I will," and then he went into the bedroom to pray. After some time, he emerged a different man. "What happened?" asked his wife. "What's come over you? Well," he said, "the Lord settled it with me. I knelt beside the bed and poured out my heart to Him. I told Him how bitter I was that the president received this tremendous homecoming, but there was no one there to meet us when we returned home. And when I finished, it seemed as though the Lord put His hand on my shoulder and simply said, 'But … you're not home yet!'"

NOTES

FOREWORD: Answering life's most painful question

1. Quoted from the introduction to the book of Job in the SourceView Bible app, which can be downloaded for free for either Apple or Android devices from their respective stores.
2. Job 42:5, New Living Translation.
3. Rev 21:4, New Living Translation.

CHAPTER ONE: There's been a shooting at the base

1. Bob VanDerVeen, Personal conversation, July 20th, 2018.
2. George Merritt, *Gunman may have warned of 2nd attack,* Associated Press, December 11, 2007.
3. Columbine High School is one of the largest public schools in the Denver-metro area, just 23 minutes to the south of the YWAM base. Eight years earlier, two students, Eric Harris and Dylan Klebold, had murdered 12 students and a teacher, as well as injuring 24 others as they tried to escape. The pair then committed suicide. At the time, the massacre was the deadliest high school shooting in US history.
4. Keeley Lange, Personal conversation, 2018
5. Stephanie Snell, Personal conversation, 2018
6. Stephen Long, Personal conversation, 2018
7. Naomi Gill, Personal conversation, 2018
8. Amanda Lange Bower, Personal conversation, 2018
9. Jisook Han, Personal conversation, 2018
10. A.J. DeAndrea, Personal conversation, 2018

CHAPTER TWO: Selfishness

1. Philip Yancey, *Where Is God When It Hurts?* p. 90
2. Winkie Pratney, *The Nature & Character of God,* p. 171
3. Ibid. p. 166

4. Kenneth S. Wuest, *Word Studies in the Greek New Testament* (Grand Rapids: Eerdmans Publishing Company, 1973), vol. 3, p. 120
5. Gregory Boyd – *God of the Possible, Pp. 134-35*
6. Billy Graham, *World Aflame*, p. 57
7. Roger Forster, *God's Strategy in Human History*, p. 244
8. Vishal Mangalwadi, *"The Book That Made Your World"*, Page 48
9. C. S. Lewis, *The Problem of Pain*, p. 96
10. U2, *Every Breaking Wave, Songs of innocence,* 2013
11. Stephen Covey, *The 7 Habits of Highly Effective People*, Pp. 38-39

CHAPTER THREE: The Fall of Man

1. C.S.Lewis, *The Problem of Pain* – p. 72
2. Roger Forster, *God's Strategy in Human History,* pp. 46-47
3. Billy Graham, *World Aflame* – Pp. 68-69
4. Mike Saia, *Why Do the Innocent Suffer?* p. 75
5. Philip Yancey, *Where Is God When It hurts?* p. 51
6. Mike Saia, *Why Do the Innocent Suffer?* p. 65
7. C.S.Lewis, *The Problem of Pain* – p. 2
8. Crosby, Stills & Nash, *Déjà Vu,* 1970
9. Plastic Ono Band, *Give Peace a Chance,* 1969
10. Philip Yancey, *Where Is God When It Hurts?* p. 67
11. Billy Graham, *World Aflame* – Page 233
12. Philip Yancey, *Where Is God When It Hurts?* p. 252
13. Peter Kreeft, *Making Sense Out of Suffering,* p. 139
14. Philip Yancey, *Where Is God When It Hurts?* p. 254
15. Ibid. p. 245

CHAPTER FOUR: The decay of the earth

1. Pietz, David (2002). *Engineering the State: The Huai River and Reconstruction in Nationalist China 1927–1937*, Routledge, p. xvii, p. 61–70
2. Mindy Berry, Personal conversation, September 23rd, 2018
3. Mike Saia, *Why Do the Innocent Suffer?* Pp. 74-75
4. Mindy Berry, Personal conversation, September 23rd, 2018

CHAPTER FIVE: Ignorance

1. Mike Saia, *Why Do the Innocent Suffer?* p. 134
2. Stephanie Snell, Personal conversation, January 15th, 2018
3. Paul Dangtoumda, personal conversation, October 18th, 2018

CHAPTER SIX: Disregard for the laws of nature

1. See John Hick, *Philosophy of Religion,* chapter 3
2. Ibid
3. C. S. Lewis, *The Problem of Pain*, p. 23
4. Philip Yancey, *Where Is God When It Hurts?* p. 65
5. Joshua Lee Bergen, personal conversation, Dec. 21st, 2017

CHAPTER SEVEN: The Kingdom of Darkness

1. John Dawson, *Taking Our Cities For God,* p. 131
2. The Rolling Stones, *Sympathy for the Devil*
3. John Dawson, *Taking Our Cities For God* – Pages 151-152
4. C. Peter Wagner, *Warfare Prayer,* p. 120-121
5. Thomas Yoder Neufeld, *Armour of God,* quoted in E. Warren, *Cleansing the Cosmos: A Biblical Model for Contextualizing Evil,* p. 219
6. C. Jung, *"Wotan," in Civilization in transition,* Collected works 10, ed. H. Read, M. Fordham and G. Adler, trans. R. F. C. Hull (New York: Pantheon, 1970), pp. 185-187
7. Walter Wink, *Unmasking the powers,* p. 54
8. John Dawson, *Taking Our Cities For God* – Page 135-136
9. Greg Boyd, *God at War* – page 12
10. Greg Boyd, *God at War* – p. 14
11. Kraft, *Understanding Spiritual Power*, p. 77-78
12. F.F. Brenk, *"In the light of the moon: Demonology in the Early Imperial Period,"* in ANRW (1986), ed. H. Temporini and W. Haase, 2/16.3.2068-2145; Also, S.S. Jensen, *Dualism and Demonology: The Function of Demonology in Pythagorean and Platonic Thought* (Copenhagen: Munksgaard, 1966
13. Greg Boyd, *God At War* – p. 18
14. John Dawson, *Taking our cities for God* – p. 153
15. David Peterson, *Engaging with God: A Biblical Theology of Worship* (Grand Rapids, Mich.: Eerdmans, 1992), Pp. 24-25
16. Gary Kinnaman, *Angels Dark and Light*, p. 164
17. Colonel L. Gordon Cooper, testifying before a sub-committee of the UN (www.gravitywarpdrive.com/UFO_Testimonies.htm #Astronautsandcosmonauts)
18. Ibid.
19. Gary Kinnaman, *Angels Dark and Light*, Pp 132-33
20. See Billy Graham, *Angels: God's secret agents*
21. G. E. Ladd, *The Presence of the Future: The Eschatology of Biblical Realism* (Grand Rapids, Mich.: Eerdmans, 1974), p. 161

22. Billy Graham, *Angels: God's Secret Agents*, p. 3

23. Gregory Boyd, *God at war*, p. 133

24. James G. Kallas, *"The Significance of the Synoptic Miracles".* Greenwich, Conn.: Seabury Press, 1961, p. 65

25. H. A. Kelley, *"The Devil at Baptism: Ritual, Theology and Drama".* Cornell University Press, 1985, p. 18

26. Mickey Hart, *Drumming at the Edge of Magic: A journey into the Spirit of Percussion* (New York: Harper Collins, 1990), Pp. 15, 180, 181

27. Greg Boyd, *Is God To Blame?* p. 71

28. J. Ramsey Michaels, *Jesus and the Unclean Spirits,* p. 50

29. Henry Hampton Halley, *Halley's Bible Handbook – Page 468*

30. Edward Langdon, *"The Essentials of Demonology: A Study of Jewish and Christian Doctrine, Its Origin and Development."* London. Epworth, 1949, pp. 171-72

CHAPTER EIGHT: God's divine testing

1. Traditionally, the apostle Paul was thought to be the author of the book of Hebrews, however, since the third century this has been questioned, and the general consensus among most modern scholars is that the author is unknown. Some suggest that Priscilla might have actually written the Epistle to the Hebrews, but her name was left off the manuscript because of the stigma of female teachers within that culture. Ruth Hoppin provides considerable support for this viewpoint, maintaining that she "meets every qualification, matches every clue, and looms ubiquitous in every line of investigation". She suggests, the masculine participle, may have been added by a scribe, or the author deliberately used a neutral participle "as a kind of abstraction" (Ruth Hoppin, "The Epistle to the Hebrews is Priscilla's Letter" in Amy-Jill Levine, Maria Mayo Robins (eds), *A Feminist Companion to the Catholic Epistles and Hebrews*, (A&C Black, 2004) pages 147-170)

2. R.C.H. Lenski, *The Interpretation of St. Paul's First and Second Epistles to the Corinthians,* Augsburg Pub. House, Minneapolis MN, 1963, p. 1332

3. Philip Yancey, *Where Is God When It Hurts?* p. 98

4. Ibid.

5. Rick Warren, *Why God Goes Quiet – Authentic Christian Leadership Devotional,* September 5th

6. Philip Yancey, *Where Is God When It Hurts?* p. 77

7. C. S. Lewis, *The Problem of Pain,* p. 111

8. Gene Edwards, *A Tale of Three Kings,* p. 12
9. The Beatles, *Blackbird,* 1968
10. David J. Garrow, *Bearing the Cross,* p. 532
11. Mike Saia, *Why Do the Innocent Suffer?* Pp. 35-37

CHAPTER NINE: God's judgments on sin

1. Klaus Koch, *Doctrine of Retribution,* p. 77
2. Ibid, Pp. 60-64
3. Mike Saia, *Why Do the Innocent Suffer?* p. 130
4. Gregory A. Boyd, *Cross Vision,* Pp. 202-03
5. Michael Gabler, Max Plank Institute for Astrophysics, *World of Knowledge,* p. 64
6. 21. Greg Boyd, *God at War,* p. 150
7. Mark S. Smith, trans. *Ugaritic Narrative Poetry,* Simon B. Parker, ed., (Atlanta: Society of Biblical Literature, 1997), 148. In the same volume see also *"Baal Fathers a Bull"* Simon B. Parker, trans., 181-186 and *"A Birth"* Simon B. Parker, trans. 186-187. W. F. Albright says that in "the light of several Egyptian accounts of the goddess, unquestionably translated from an original Canaanite myth" that Baal raped Anath while she was in the form of a calf. W. F. Albright, Yahweh and the God's of Canaan: A Historical Analysis of Two Contrasting Faiths (Winona Lake, IN: Eisenbrauns, 1968), 128-129
8. C. S. Lewis, *The Problem of Pain,* Pp. 127-28
9. Sandra L. Richter, *The Deuteronomistic History and the Name Theology: le šakkēn šemô šām in the Bible and the Ancient Near East* (Berlin/New York: Walter de Gruyter, 2002

CHAPTER TEN: When God doesn't intervene

1. www.nytimes.com/aponline/arts/AP-People-Turner.html, April 16, 2001
2. The word infinite means "unlimited"
3. Dean Sherman, *Spiritual Warfare for every Christian,* p. 128
4. Aurelius Augustine, *City of God* 5. 10; NPNF 2:93
5. Roger Forster, *God's Strategy in Human History,* p. 27
6. Vishal Mangalwadi, *The Book That Made Your World,* p. 239
7. Roger Forster, *God's Strategy in Human History,* p. 28
8. Mike Saia, *Why Do the Innocent Suffer? p.* 98
9. Roger Forster, *God's Strategy in Human History,* Pp. 35-36
10. Ibid. p. 36

11. Ibid. p. 244
12. Gordon Olson, *The Moral Government of God*, Pp. 14-15
13. Ibid. Pp. 14-15
14. C. S. Lewis, *The Problem of Pain*, p. 130
15. Gregory Boyd, *Is God To Blame?* p. 63
16. Roger Forster, *God's Strategy in Human History*, p. 28
17. Dean Sherman, *Spiritual Warfare for every Christian*, p. 129
18. W.A. Pratney, *The Nature And Character Of God*, p. 183
19. Charles Finney, *Systematic Theology*, p.1
20. W. A. Pratney, *The Nature And Character Of God*, p. 184
21. Gordon Olson, *The Moral Government of God*, p. 12
22. Billy Graham, *World Aflame*, p. 87
23. Vishal Mangalwadi, *The Book That Made Your World*, p. 336
24. "Rule of law" is the restriction of the arbitrary exercise of power by subordinating it to well-defined and established laws
25. W.A. Pratney, *The Nature and Character of God*, p. 441
26. C.S. Lewis, *The Lion, the Witch and the Wardrobe*, p. 141-142

CHAPTER ELEVEN: Those who give their lives

1. Janet & Geoff Benge, *Nate Saint: On a Wing and a Prayer*, Pp. 183–84
2. See Charisma Magazine, *Are you all in?*
3. What a Beautiful Name, *Hillsong Worship*, 2016
4. N.T. Wright, *The Day The Revolution Began*, p. 366
5. Philip Yancey, *Where Is God When It Hurts*, p. 77
6. N. T. Wright, *The Day The Revolution Began*, p. 375
7. Margaret Clarkson, So Send I You, 1954

Peter Warren

Connect with Peter

Peter and the team at YWAM Denver would love to hear from you! Whether you're interested in short term missions or have a question about the topics addressed in this book, we're available!

Peter has taught in churches, conferences, and YWAM schools for over 30 years. In addition to the issue of God and suffering, he speaks widely on Missions, Worship, Spiritual Warfare, and understanding God's character. Please connect with us if you would be interested in having him speak at your event.

peterwarren@ywamdenver.org
Peterwarrenministries.com

Instagram & Facebook
@YWAMDenver
ywamdenver.org